# SHATTERED BONDS
## A BROTHER'S BETRAYAL

## LAMAR B. BURNO SR.

# Table of Contents

# Synopsis

Shattered Bonds: A Brother's Betrayal is the gripping true story of Lamar Burno Sr., a decorated martial artist, executive protection specialist, and devoted father, who was betrayed by the very person he trusted most: his own identical twin brother.

What begins as a tale of family loyalty and shared dreams spirals into a harrowing journey of false accusations, devastating lies, and a battle to reclaim dignity, justice, and mental peace. Set against a backdrop of courtroom corruption, spiritual warfare, and raw emotional pain, Lamar's story exposes the dark side of envy, the abuse of legal systems, and the generational trauma that silence often conceals.

But this isn't just a story of betrayal, it's one of survival. With unshakable faith, support from unexpected allies, and a warrior's heart, Lamar rises from the ashes to become a voice for truth, mental health awareness, and personal redemption.

This book isn't just a memoir, it's a movement. Shattered Bonds will leave you inspired, outraged, and deeply moved.

**Dr. Michael Neely, PhD**

CEO of New Praise Music Group, Pastor, and Music Consultant

"Because Lamar encouraged me to remain focused and committed to purpose, I now hold an Honorary PhD in Music Philosophy. His impact on my life is undeniable. This book reflects the strength, pain, and purpose of a man called by destiny."

**Marc Nelson**

Platinum Recording Artist, Founding Member of Boyz II Men, Lead Singer of Az Yet

"Lamar Burno Sr. is not just a brother he's a warrior, a protector, and a survivor. His story is one the world needs to hear. I've watched him overcome things that would've crushed most men. This book isn't just powerful, it's necessary. Lamar's strength, courage, tenacity and his willingness to help anyone makes him a rare breed. He's going to be the next LA Reid with his Management skills. I'm proud to be your Siu Lum Pai Brother."

**SiFu Rome**

Grandmaster, Hung Gar Kung Fu – The Shaolin Experience

"Lamar has trained under me for years and carries the discipline, loyalty, and power that martial arts teaches at its highest level. His journey is the embodiment of inner strength. I stand behind him as both a student and a man of integrity."

# Dedication

To my business partners Damascene, Kevin and Cedric — we're on our way to the top…!

To Michael Angelo, Michael Graziano, Joe Sarnese, and Stephen Romeo Sr— thank you for embracing me in the Italian community.

To my brothers from another mother Bryant Pugh, Shango Jamal, Moses Mason III, Mark Small, Marc Nelson, FW Newton, Flame Newton, Michael Neely, John Ross Jr., Ron Murray, Eddie Davis Jr., Fletcher Collins, Randy Smith and Tom Damus — thanks for holding me down through rough times.

To my parents, Kenneth H. Burno Sr. and Dorothy Burno — thank you for your sacrifices, love, and guidance that shaped me into the man I am.

To my bonus mom, Annette — your kindness, warmth, and love have always meant the world to me.

To my siblings, Kenneth Burno Jr. and Tiffany Burno — your presence in my life is priceless.

To my bonus siblings — Jesse, Veronica, and Eric — family is not just blood, it's bond. I appreciate each of you.

To my daughter, Alexis Hall — and my grandsons, DeAnte Jr. and Bryson — you are my pride, my joy, and my reason to keep rising.

To my son-in-law, DeAnte Sr. — thank you for being a solid man and a loving father.

To my nieces, Keonni and Ariana— Uncle loves you dearly. Watching you grow has brought me immense joy.

To my nephew, Brandon — I love you and appreciate your support more than you know.

To my sister-in-law, Felicia and brother in law, Eric— your encouragement throughout this process has truly lifted my spirit.

To my cherished grandparents — Rev. Luther and Princess Cooper, and

Timothy and Mary Burno — your memory lives within every step I take. This book is dedicated to your prayers and legacy.

To my spiritual parents- Apostle and Mother Goode, thank you for your unwavering spiritual covering.

To my rock, Genise — your love, patience, and quiet strength anchor me. I see you. I value you. I thank God for you.

To Consuela Hipsher — my editing angel. Your belief in this project, and in me, helped bring this vision to life. I'll never forget your support.

To my aunts, uncles, bonus nieces and nephews, and all of my artists signed to Burno-Patterson Entertainment — your trust, talent, and time are appreciated more than you know.

To everyone who's ever crossed my path — thank you for shaping my journey.


To the people who believed the lies spread by Monte — may this book open your eyes to the truth. Your judgment fueled my determination to rise, and I forgive you.

To my martial arts instructors — SiFu Rome (Hung Gar Kung Fu), Sensei Madison Nelson (Tae Kwon Do), and Cornelius Graper (13 Star Pattern Ninjitsu) — you molded the fighter and protector in me. Thank you for the discipline and the honor.

To my Dream Team of Attorneys — your fight, your fire, and your faith in justice gave me the strength to keep going. Thank you for standing with me in truth and honor.

To all my students — continue to walk in power, humility, and integrity. The legacy you build begins with the principles you uphold.

And finally,

To everyone who ever believed in me — this book is part of our victory.

## Special Dedications

To My Pastor and God Brother, Dr. Jamal Harrison Bryant

Your life, your voice, and your bold walk in truth have inspired millions — but for me, it's personal. You've been more than a pastor. You've been a brother, a mentor, a lifeline, and a reflection of God's grace under pressure. In moments when I was ready to give up, your sermons revived me. When the lies were loud, your truth was louder. You covered me spiritually when I didn't have the strength to cover myself emotionally.

You've led with courage, preached with conviction, and stood firm in the face of opposition. Watching you rise in ministry while staying rooted in humility gave me the blueprint to survive my own storm. This book carries my truth, but your influence is in every chapter. Your anointing has reminded me that even betrayal has a purpose, and that God always has the final say.

Thank you for being a real one. A kingdom builder. A general in the army of the Lord. And most of all, my brother by both spirit and assignment.

This is our victory too. With deepest honor, Lamar Burno Sr.

To Danette Vercher

Thank you for being the light in the shadows, the truth in the confusion, and the strength behind the scenes. Your courage to speak up and provide visual evidence brought a level of clarity to this book that cannot be overstated. You didn't just support me — you helped validate my truth when others tried to erase it.

In a time when silence would've been safer, you chose to stand with integrity. Your contribution helped expose deception and protect legacy. Because of you, lies were shattered and the truth was finally given a voice. You reminded me that real loyalty isn't loud, it's consistent.

Danette, this book is not just a story of survival — it's a document of redemption, and your fingerprints are on every breakthrough moment.

Thank you for your trust, your strength, and your unwavering belief in what's right.
You helped bring the light. With gratitude and honor, Lamar Burno Sr.

**Special Thanks**

To Michael Rivers

Thank you for your steadfast legal support and unwavering presence. You

were more than just counsel — you were the brother I could call on anytime. In moments of chaos, your calm, wisdom, and loyalty stood strong. I am grateful for your belief in me, your fight for justice, and your friendship that never wavered.
You didn't just represent me, you stood with me. With deep respect and gratitude,

Lamar Burno Sr.

# Chapter 1

## Same Face, Different Spirit

"For a man's enemies will be the members of his own household." – Matthew 10:36 (NASB)

We came into this world together, two souls bound by birth, sharing the same womb, the same birthday, and the same DNA. Monte and I were identical twins, but over time, it became clear that while our faces matched, our spirits could not have been more different. From the outside, it may have appeared that we were a team, brothers who had each other's backs. But behind closed doors, a deeper, darker truth unfolded—a truth masked by the phrase we heard all too often: "What goes on in this house, stays in this house."

That phrase, often spoken in Black households like ours, was supposed to protect our family from shame. Instead, it became a cage that trapped pain, silenced cries for help, and kept mental illness hidden behind a veil of secrecy. My brother Monte was battling demons that none of us could see clearly at first. What began as jealousy and resentment soon evolved into manipulation, lies, and destructive behaviors aimed at me—his own twin.

There were moments when I tried to make sense of his behavior. I wanted to believe that he loved me deep down, that his actions came from a place of pain, not hatred. But love does not try to destroy. Love does not lie on your name, sabotage your opportunities, or send anonymous letters to law enforcement to ruin your reputation. Monte did all of that and more. He weaponized our bloodline. He made me his enemy.

Throughout the years, I have watched him wear different masks, manipulating everyone around him while playing the victim. He inserted himself into court cases that had nothing to do with him. He forged false narratives, even trying to paint me as a felon in multiple states—all out of bitterness that I had moved forward while he remained stuck in the mirror, fighting the man he refused to become.

Monte's jealousy began early. If I was recognized, he felt ignored. If I was praised, he felt invisible. Instead of drawing inspiration from our shared experiences, he used every accomplishment I reached as a reason to tear me down. It didn't matter whether it was in martial arts, law enforcement, entertainment, or ministry. If I walked through the door first, Monte made it his mission to make sure I tripped along the way.

There was a time when I made excuses for him. I told myself, He's just hurt. He needs help. But the truth is, no amount of hurt gives someone the right to be hateful. When Monte began lying to pastors, law enforcement, and even our own family about me, I knew I had to draw a line—not out of revenge, but for survival. I loved my brother, but I could not let him destroy me.

The deepest betrayal doesn't come from enemies; it comes from the ones who share your blood, your history, and your home.
Monte and I came from the same place, but we chose drastically different paths. I chose healing, discipline, and God. Monte chose deception, instability, and a spirit of confusion. I do not say this to shame him, but to bring light to what so many families hide in the shadows.

Mental illness in our communities is often left untreated. It is dismissed as mood swings, attitude problems, or spiritual warfare. But what happens when untreated trauma becomes a weapon?
What happens when a brother turns into a lifelong antagonist? What happens when the man who shares your face becomes the person trying hardest to erase your legacy?

This chapter is not written in anger. It is written in truth. Truth that frees. Truth that heals. Truth that breaks the generational curse of silence. Monte may be my twin, but he does not define me. His actions do not dictate my destiny. I am more than the lies he told. I am more than the pain he caused. I am a survivor of sibling betrayal, and this is my story.

The journey ahead is filled with painful memories, shocking revelations, and spiritual lessons. But it begins here—with two brothers born the same day, walking two very different roads. One chasing healing, the other running from himself.

In the end, this story is not just about betrayal. It is about rising above it. It is about reclaiming your name, your voice, and your peace. And for anyone reading this who has ever been betrayed by family—know that you are not alone. Your pain has a purpose. And your purpose can lead to power.

# Chapter 2

## The Face in the Mirror

"But if you harbor bitter envy and selfish ambition in your hearts, do not boast about it or deny the truth." – James 3:14 (NIV)

Growing up, Monte and I were often dressed alike. Our mother would style our hair the same, buy us matching outfits, and introduce us as "the twins" everywhere we went. From the outside, it looked like unity. To strangers, we were one person duplicated. But even as a child, I began to sense the difference between us. I would look at him and feel like I was staring at a mirror that reflected something slightly off, a version of me that didn't want to smile unless he was winning.

There were subtle moments in our youth that revealed how deeply Monte battled with comparison. If I got a compliment, he would find a way to dismiss it. If I won an award, he would act as though he deserved it more. I didn't want to compete with my own brother. I wanted us to succeed together, but it was clear early on that Monte didn't want to stand beside me. He wanted to stand above me.

Jealousy isn't always loud. Sometimes it shows up in the small things. Monte would take credit for things I accomplished. If I trained harder in martial arts and placed in a tournament, he'd tell people he coached me. If someone complimented my discipline, he'd insert a story about his leadership. It wasn't just sibling rivalry. It was a growing obsession with proving he was better, even if it meant lying.

As we got older, the divide deepened. I invested in myself. I pushed through hardships and took accountability for my growth. Monte seemed stuck, unable to accept that effort brings results. Instead of growing with me, he grew bitter. That bitterness began to bleed into everything. His words. His actions. His treatment of our family. Especially me.

It wasn't just that Monte was envious. It was that he couldn't handle my success without feeling like it diminished him. He believed every blessing I received was a reflection of his failure. He took my progress personally. That level of jealousy is toxic, and when it comes from someone with your same blood, it becomes even more dangerous. Because that person knows your strengths, your dreams, and your weaknesses.

There were times I reached out to help him. I offered opportunities. I invited him into business ventures. I even gave him positions in my security company. But each time, he used those bridges as launching pads for betrayal. He would smile in front of others, then lie behind closed doors. I had to learn the hard way that not everyone deserves access to your journey, even if they share your last name.

Monte saw me as his competition, not his brother. And I realized that no matter how much I tried to love him through it, I couldn't change the face he saw in the mirror. He wasn't angry at me. He was angry at himself. I was just the easiest target.

You can't heal someone who doesn't want healing. You can't force peace with someone who thrives on chaos. And you can't carry someone who's trying to pull you down while pretending to lift you up. Monte was drowning in envy, and I had to stop jumping in after him.

The most painful part of it all was realizing that I had to protect myself from someone who looked just like me. I wasn't dealing with a stranger. I was facing a version of myself that chose resentment over redemption.

This chapter is not about casting blame. It's about confronting the silent war that happens when one sibling becomes the villain in the other's story. It's about acknowledging that sometimes the person you want to save is the one who wants to see you fall.

I stopped asking why he hated me. I stopped trying to earn his respect. And I stopped chasing his love. I began to focus on healing the parts of me that were wounded by his betrayal. I turned to God. I turned to purpose. I turned to peace.

There is power in letting go. There is freedom in saying, "I'm not your enemy, but I'm no longer your victim." And there is strength in understanding that not everyone who shares your face shares your spirit.

Monte chose bitterness. I chose to break free.

# Chapter 3

## When Silence Covers Storms

"Even my close friend in whom I trusted, who ate my bread, has lifted up his heel against me." – Psalm 41:9 (NASB)

S ome betrayals don't begin with a knife in the back. They begin with small silences, moments where truth should have spoken, but didn't. Monte and I were raised in a home that believed in discipline, pride, and the unspoken code of "family first." But beneath that structure was a brewing storm that no one wanted to acknowledge, Monte's growing instability.

In our house, being emotional was considered weak. Expressing confusion or mental strain was almost forbidden. When Monte showed signs of anger, resentment, or depression, it was chalked up to "just having a bad day." But those bad days became patterns, and those patterns became personality. He would fly into rage when corrected, manipulate stories to avoid accountability, and isolate himself after any moment of correction or failure.

As a child, I watched him throw tantrums that would turn violent. I watched him blame others for things he clearly did. When we were kids, two separate psychologists recommended that Monte be placed on medication to help regulate his behavior. But our mother, being deeply spiritual, believed in prayer over pills. She did what she thought was right. She loved him. But love alone couldn't cure what was happening in his mind.

Monte's behavior only grew more toxic with age. He developed a habit of rewriting reality to make himself look like a victim or a hero, never the cause. If he got fired, the boss was racist. If a relationship failed, the woman was cheating. If someone called him out, they were jealous. It didn't matter what the truth was. His version of events always placed him at the center of injustice, no matter how much destruction he left behind.

And while he was spinning tales, I stayed quiet. For years, I held back the truth because I didn't want to be seen as attacking my own blood. I believed in protecting family, in guarding the image of unity even when there was no peace behind the scenes. I silenced my own pain to avoid airing Monte's behavior publicly.
That silence nearly destroyed me.

Monte's first major explosion came during a family hunting trip. We were in the woods, early morning. I had fallen asleep in the passenger seat while he was driving. Later, he confessed that he held his loaded 9mm to my head while I slept. He told me the only reason he didn't pull the trigger was because he didn't want to hurt our mother. I was stunned. Numb. What do you do with a confession like that? How do you process knowing that your own twin brother contemplated murdering you?

Even then, I didn't tell anyone. I brushed it off, compartmentalized it, and filed it in a box marked "Do not open." But silence doesn't make the truth disappear. It only lets the poison spread quietly.

I began to realize that Monte had been at war with me long before that moment in the car. That hunting trip wasn't the beginning. It was the culmination of years of unchecked resentment. He hated the reflection of himself that he saw when I walked in purpose. He despised how I kept rising no matter what life threw at me. He hated that I didn't crumble under the pressure the way he did.

Family didn't see what I saw. They saw his charm. They saw his manners when he wanted to impress. But I saw the aftermath, the trail of people he left broken, confused, or betrayed once he no longer needed them. I saw the manipulation, the twisting of facts, the calculated lies. And when I finally decided to start speaking up, I became his target.

Monte didn't want peace. He wanted pity. And when I stopped being silent, I took away his ability to use me as the villain in his stories.

The truth is, I don't hate my brother. I grieve him. I grieve the version of us that could have been. I grieve the brotherhood that was never truly real because it was built on my silence and his sabotage.

Silence might protect the storm for a while, but eventually, the damage reaches the surface. And when it does, healing can finally begin. That's why I'm telling this story, not to shame, but to shine a light on what many people are afraid to say.

If you have ever protected someone at the cost of your own peace, let this be a reminder: you are not obligated to carry someone else's chaos. You have a right to your truth. You have a right to speak it.

And now, I am.

# Chapter 4

## The Betrayal of Blood

"Can two walk together, unless they are agreed?" – Amos 3:3 (NKJV)

There is a weight that comes with being betrayed by a stranger, but there is a deeper sting when that betrayal comes from someone who shares your blood. Monte and I entered the world together, yet it often felt like I was walking life's path alone. At some point, I realized we weren't just twins. We were two men raised in the same house, but walking in two completely different directions.

I always believed that blood should mean loyalty, but Monte saw it differently. To him, being my twin was less about brotherhood and more about leverage. He used our connection as a way to gain trust with people, only to twist that trust into opportunity for sabotage. He positioned himself in places I had already paved, then tore at the very foundation I had built. To this day, I believe he never wanted what I had. He wanted to destroy what I built so that neither of us could stand.

What kind of person does that? Someone battling with identity. Someone who sees your reflection as a threat instead of a reminder of shared roots. Monte didn't just want success. He wanted to be seen as the "real" twin. The one who came out on top. But in doing so, he abandoned every principle of brotherhood.

I tried to ignore it. I told myself that maybe he would grow out of it. That maybe, with time, the jealousy would fade. But instead of maturing, Monte became more calculated. He spread lies about me to family, friends, and even to law enforcement. When I started gaining ground in my professional life, he made it his mission to strip me of credibility. He called agencies. He sent anonymous letters. He slandered my name and said I was a fraud. He tried to turn my victories into violations.

But here is what Monte never understood. My journey wasn't built on hype or shortcuts. It was built on discipline, faith, and favor. Every door that opened for me came through blood, sweat, prayer, and purpose. And that kind of favor can't be canceled by a jealous twin with a pen.

One of the most defining moments came when I was working to become certified in law enforcement. Monte had applied years earlier and was denied for not meeting the requirements. But when I went through the process, passed all investigations, and completed the fast-track training course, Monte lost control. He falsely reported me to the Florida Department of Law Enforcement and even sent an anonymous letter pretending to be a church bishop. His goal was clear, stop me before I could succeed. He didn't care about truth. He cared about control.

What kind of man pretends to be a bishop to destroy his own brother's future? That's not just envy. That's spiritual sickness. That's a heart consumed with pride, bitterness, and delusion.

And even with all of that, I never struck back. I never called the authorities on him. I never tried to ruin his name. I stayed silent for far too long, hoping he would change. But silence isn't loyalty when it enables abuse. And peace isn't peace if it costs you your sanity.

Monte didn't just betray me. He betrayed our legacy. He mocked our parents' values. He disrespected the opportunities we both were given. He didn't just fall out with me. He fell out with his own destiny. And all I could do was watch, pray, and keep walking.

I've learned that blood does not make someone family. Loyalty does. Honor does. Respect does. And when those things are broken repeatedly, you must protect yourself. Not with hate, but with boundaries. Not with revenge, but with truth.

I stopped asking Monte to walk beside me. I stopped trying to drag him into a future he wasn't willing to fight for. I forgave him, but I refused to let him back into the parts of my life that required integrity, peace, and trust.

The betrayal of blood is not just painful. It's sobering. It teaches you who you are and what you will no longer tolerate. I chose to live. I chose to lead. I chose to break the cycle. And I chose to write this so that someone else can recognize the signs and make a decision before the damage becomes permanent.

This chapter isn't about bitterness. It's about boundaries. It's about realizing that not everyone tied to your origin is meant to be part of your outcome.

# Chapter 5

## The Puppet Master

"The heart is deceitful above all things, and desperately wicked. Who can understand it?" – Jeremiah 17:9 (NIV)

Monte wasn't just jealous. He was strategic. Over time, I realized I wasn't dealing with a confused brother trying to find his way. I was dealing with a manipulator. A master of control. A puppet master who thrived on playing everyone against each other while hiding his own hand.

He knew how to smile at people while setting traps behind their backs. He would act concerned in public, then twist narratives in private. I watched him carefully craft situations where he could control the outcome. If things didn't go his way, he'd rewrite the story to make himself the victim and everyone else the enemy.

For years, I blamed myself. I questioned whether I had unintentionally hurt him. I asked God if there was something I missed, some moment where I failed him as a brother. But the truth was, Monte wasn't interested in reconciliation. He was addicted to control. He wanted to orchestrate every narrative and remain at the center of sympathy.

Monte made it his mission to insert himself into situations that didn't involve him, and when I drew boundaries, he accused me of being disloyal. He couldn't stand the idea of me moving forward without him. Not because he wanted to walk beside me, but because he couldn't control the direction anymore.

I gave him chances. Too many, if I'm honest. I gave him roles in my business. I included him in family events. I offered him resources to better his life. But each time I opened a door, he used it as a vantage point to observe, sabotage, and twist the facts to his advantage. He would take fragments of truth, sprinkle them with lies, and sell them to whoever would listen.

At one point, Monte told others that I had stolen his identity. He claimed I forged documents, took his achievements, and profited off his name. These were bold lies that had no basis in fact. But that didn't stop him from filing reports, contacting agencies, and feeding fabricated stories to anyone who would entertain his delusion.

And while he was orchestrating chaos, I was working. Building. Earning real respect from real people. I was putting in the hours, managing artists, handling protection assignments, creating businesses, and making a name for myself based on merit. But Monte couldn't see that. All he saw was my success as a threat to his fantasy of being "the better twin."

Monte didn't want me to succeed without his involvement. If he couldn't control the narrative, he'd try to burn down the stage. And when I refused to react, he escalated. He contacted my jobs. He called the police. He filed false accusations. All to gain attention. All to make himself seem like the victim of a story he was writing in real time.

I wasn't just dealing with sibling rivalry. I was surviving psychological warfare. A campaign rooted in envy, masked by family ties.

The saddest part is that Monte is intelligent. He's capable. But instead of using his talents to build something of his own, he chose to tear down mine. Not because it benefited him, but because he couldn't stand the thought of me rising higher than the fantasy he had created in his mind.

It took years for me to understand that some people are not fighting you because you wronged them. They are fighting you because your existence confronts the truth they're unwilling to face.

Monte could never be content because he never faced his own reflection. And as long as he refused to heal, he remained a puppet master trapped in his own web, controlling lies while losing reality.

This chapter is not about exposing Monte. It's about freeing myself from the strings. I no longer move to the pull of his accusations. I no longer dance to the guilt of being the stronger twin. I no longer apologize for becoming the man I was destined to be.

Freedom isn't just the absence of conflict. It's the presence of clarity. And I finally see Monte for who he is. Not with hate. But with truth.

# Chapter 6

## The Opposing Side

"A brother wronged is more unyielding than a fortified city. Disputes are like the barred gates of a citadel." – Proverbs 18:19 (NIV)

There's a different kind of pain that comes when your own brother shows up in court, not to stand by your side, but to sit with those who want to see you fall. Monte didn't just turn his back on me. He became an enemy to my progress, using the courtroom as a stage for his bitterness.

Throughout my life, I've faced legal battles. Some were rooted in truth, others in false accusations. But in each one, Monte found a way to insert himself, not as a witness for me, but as a supporter of those trying to bring me down. He didn't care about justice. He cared about watching me squirm. He wanted to be there when I stumbled, so he could pretend he had the moral high ground.

There's a reason I stopped trusting easily. Monte had a pattern of cozying up to my opponents, feeding them information, offering documents, and acting like the concerned brother who only wanted the truth to come out. But truth was never his priority. Revenge was. He used the courtroom as a weapon, not a place of resolution.

When I was falsely accused in Florida, Monte was the one whispering in the background. He called departments, he sent anonymous complaints, and he reached out to prosecutors, claiming he had "inside information." What he really had was a vendetta. He knew the system could be manipulated, and he used that knowledge to try to break me down.

Instead of focusing on his own life, Monte made a career out of trying to dismantle mine. Every hearing, every filing, every motion,

16

there was a shadow. His presence lingered even when he wasn't in the building, because I knew what he had done behind the scenes. And when I looked back at the case files, I saw it clear as day—he had aligned himself with people who had no love for me.

This wasn't justice. This was sabotage disguised as concern. And the courts, not knowing the depth of his obsession, welcomed him as if he were credible. But I knew better. I knew that the man sitting on the other side of the courtroom was my own brother, hiding behind paperwork and legal jargon, praying that I would fall.

I tried to give him the benefit of the doubt. I hoped maybe one day he'd wake up and realize the damage he caused. But each time I extended grace, he responded with another knife. Another call. Another lie. Another attempt to drag my name through the dirt.

What Monte failed to realize is that I wasn't alone. I had God. I had truth. I had evidence. I had strength. And I had witnesses who could confirm that I wasn't the criminal he claimed I was.
When you live clean, your life becomes your defense. And though the enemy may lie, time always reveals the truth.

Monte wanted me to fold. He wanted to be the reason I gave up. But I used every attempt to destroy me as fuel. I studied harder. I worked smarter. I moved in silence and let my results speak louder than his rumors. He couldn't understand how I kept getting up after each attack. That's because he didn't know who was holding me up.

The hardest part wasn't fighting the system. It was fighting the betrayal. Knowing that my own blood would side with my enemies broke something in me. But it also built something stronger. Resilience. Discernment. Boundaries.

Monte thought the courtroom would be his victory lap. But in the end, it became my proving ground. He lost the moment he stepped out of brotherhood and into bitterness. And I won not because I beat him, but because I refused to become like him.

This chapter isn't about courtrooms. It's about courage. The courage to stand when even your family wants to see you fall. The courage to speak truth when lies surround you. And the courage to keep rising when the people closest to you try to pull you under.

I didn't lose. I learned. And now, I know exactly who belongs beside me in battle—and who belongs behind the barricade.

# Chapter 7

## The Name He Couldn't Carry

"A good name is more desirable than great riches; to be esteemed is better than silver or gold." – Proverbs 22:1 (NIV)

There came a moment when Monte made it official. He changed his last name. The explanation he gave to others was vague and dramatic. He claimed it was because someone had stolen his identity. But the truth, the one he never wanted to confront, was much deeper. Monte wasn't running from theft. He was running from himself.

Changing a last name isn't something people do lightly. It's symbolic. It's permanent. It's personal. When Monte made that decision, I knew it wasn't about protection. It was about rejection. He rejected who he was, who we were, and who I had become. He no longer wanted to be associated with my name because in his mind, that name represented everything he failed to become.

The Burno name wasn't perfect, but it carried history. It carried legacy. Our father built his reputation in the streets and in the neighborhood as a man of strength, discipline, and honor. I worked hard to elevate that name through law enforcement, martial arts, security, business, and entertainment. I made it a name that carried weight. A name that opened doors. Monte couldn't bear that, because the name reminded him of everything he walked away from.

When he changed his name, he thought it was a declaration of independence. In truth, it was a silent surrender. He no longer wanted to be compared to me, so instead of rising to his own potential, he tried to erase the connection altogether.

But changing your name doesn't change your story. It doesn't erase the choices you made. It doesn't reset your failures or rewrite your past. It just exposes your desire to run rather than rise.

Monte didn't understand that the problem wasn't the name. The problem was the identity crisis he never resolved. He wanted respect without responsibility. He wanted a platform without the process. And when life didn't hand him what he thought he deserved, he blamed everyone else—including me.

There were times I pitied him. Times I wanted to pull him back and remind him that it's never too late to heal, to rebuild, to return. But he didn't want restoration. He wanted reinvention. A new name. A new story. A new image that had no accountability attached.

Monte told people I was the reason he changed his name. That I stole his reputation. That I used his identity to climb ladders that he built. But what ladders? What foundations? What work? I had the receipts. The certifications. The relationships. The results. Monte had stories, theories, and accusations with no substance to back them up.

The name change wasn't a move toward truth. It was a retreat from it. He couldn't carry the Burno name because it came with expectation, with reputation, with legacy. And he knew he hadn't honored any of it.

It hurt to see my own twin brother reject a name that meant something to me. Not because I needed his approval, but because I knew what it really meant. It meant he had given up. Not just on me, but on himself.

This chapter isn't just about names. It's about identity. The kind that can't be changed by paperwork or pronunciation. True identity comes from within. From the choices we make. The integrity we carry. The legacy we honor.

I didn't choose to be better. I chose to be whole. I chose to carry the weight of our family name and turn it into something meaningful. Monte chose to let it go, hoping that a new signature could free him from the reflection in the mirror.

But no matter what name he writes, the truth will always follow.

# Chapter 8

## Ordained But Not Anointed

"Not everyone who says to Me, 'Lord, Lord,' will enter the kingdom of heaven, but only the one who does the will of My Father who is in heaven." – Matthew 7:21 (NIV)

On October 8, 2006, I watched something unfold in a church that should have been sacred. Monte was scheduled to be ordained as an Elder at Faith United Church of the Living God. But there was a problem. No one moved. No one said anything. The ordination service stalled while everyone sat in silence. For fifteen long minutes, not a single church leader made a motion to begin the process.

I wasn't even a member of that church. Yet I felt the shame of the moment. The awkward stillness was loud, like heaven itself had paused. Out of respect for our mother, who had been a faithful member, I stood up and made the motion myself. A few minutes later, my girlfriend, also not a member, seconded it.

Only then did the Bishop proceed.

Monte didn't realize it then, but that moment said everything. He wasn't chosen by the church. He was tolerated. And only because of our mother's dedication. His elevation was not led by reverence. It was prompted by embarrassment. He wanted the title, but he hadn't earned the trust. He wanted the robe, but not the responsibility. And while others clapped, I sat quietly, knowing the truth.

Over the next few years, Monte used that title recklessly. He tried to use it as leverage in arguments. He judged others harshly. He acted as though being an Elder made him spiritually superior. But the fruit of his life said otherwise. You can be ordained by men and still not be called by God.

In 2010, the truth caught up. Monte was stripped of the title of Elder after causing division at a major convocation. He tried to sabotage other preachers, questioning their credentials, whispering lies to church leaders, and making a scene that brought shame, not glory, to the ministry. The Senior Bishop had seen enough. The same church that tolerated him eventually rejected him.

Monte never recovered from that fall. He talked about it with bitterness, blaming everyone but himself. He told others the church was jealous of his anointing. He said they feared his calling. But it wasn't fear that removed him. It was fruit. Or lack of it.

There is a difference between being called and being craving. Monte craved attention. He craved titles. He craved public affirmation. But ministry isn't about spotlight. It's about sacrifice. It's about character behind closed doors. It's about loving people more than platform.

I saw how he treated people. I heard the things he said in private. His words weren't seasoned with grace. His actions weren't grounded in humility. He wore the title like a costume, hoping it would mask the brokenness inside.

I never mocked him for losing that title. I mourned. Because it was another example of Monte wanting to appear holy without doing the internal work. He could have used that opportunity to grow, to repent, to rebuild. But he used it as another weapon against others, another way to play the victim.

Spiritual abuse is real. And when people like Monte are given authority without accountability, they hurt more than themselves. They damage the very souls they claim to lead.

I've been far from perfect. But I've walked my journey with integrity. When God elevates, He does it in a way that no man can manipulate or destroy. Titles don't define me. Purpose does. And I've learned that it's better to be anointed in silence than ordained for show.

Monte wanted the appearance of being chosen. But when tested, he failed. Not because he was hated, but because he was hollow. You can't fake the Spirit. Eventually, the truth rises.

This chapter is a reminder that not everyone with a title is walking in truth. Be careful who you follow. And be even more careful who you let lay hands on you.

# Chapter 9

## Clout Over Character

"For if anyone thinks himself to be something, when he is nothing, he deceives himself." – Galatians 6:3 (NKJV)

Monte was never content with who he was. Instead of focusing on character, he chased clout. He needed people to believe he was bigger than life, even if that meant building his reputation on a stack of lies. And not just small lies, but grand, almost delusional ones that only someone detached from reality could say with a straight face.

He once told people that Jay-Z and Beyoncé bought him a Rolls Royce. He shared the story like it was common knowledge, casually inserting it into conversations as if it were just another Tuesday in his superstar lifestyle. No documentation. No photos. No event to verify. Just a bold claim told enough times that he convinced himself it was true.

The lie wasn't about the car. It was about identity. Monte wanted to appear as though he was connected, important, and envied. If I bought a luxury vehicle or achieved something, he had to outshine it, even if only in fantasy. He wasn't competing in real life. He was competing in imagination.

He claimed to be a high-ranking officer in the Guardian Angels, despite never being anything more than a member. I, on the other hand, had actually been promoted to Training Officer and eventually Executive Director under Curtis Sliwa himself. I was responsible for organizing, leading, and overseeing public safety initiatives in multiple cities. Monte? He wore a beret and acted important, but the paperwork said otherwise.

He lied about having relationships with celebrities. He pretended he was doing business deals with industry giants. He even stole parts of my resume and used them in his own biography. And when people started asking questions, he blamed me. Said I was jealous. Said I was bitter. Said I was the liar. All while standing in the shadow of my actual accomplishments.

Monte never understood that true success is not loud. It doesn't need to scream or fabricate. It simply exists. And when you've really put in the work, your fruit will speak louder than your mouth ever could.

He started fabricating news articles, even creating a fake headline claiming that I stole his identity. He posted it online, hoping to damage my reputation. But it backfired. People who knew me well laughed at the effort. They knew my work, my service, and my history. Monte looked desperate, not credible.

What he didn't expect was that all his false accusations would eventually be used as proof of his instability. Law enforcement, court officials, and my employers started to see the pattern. I didn't have to defend myself. Monte exposed himself.

But even then, I wasn't angry. I was saddened. Saddened that my own brother was so deeply lost in his identity that he had to create false stories to feel relevant. I had tried to pull him up. I gave him opportunities. I offered him a seat at the table. But he didn't want a seat. He wanted the table without the work it took to build it.

This chapter isn't about image. It's about substance. You can't Photoshop purpose. You can't fabricate favor. Eventually, clout fades. But character, that lasts.

Monte built his world on borrowed identities, stolen words, and imaginary status. I built mine on truth, consistency, and accountability. That's why his world crumbled and mine stood strong.

Your name means nothing if your life doesn't back it up. And when the spotlight fades, only your character will remain.

# Chapter 10

## The Crash That Spoke Volumes

"Do not be deceived: God is not mocked. For whatever a man sows, that he will also reap." – Galatians 6:7 (NKJV)

There are moments in life that don't need explanation. They speak for themselves. One of those moments came the day Monte crashed his Maxima into my Mercedes. It wasn't an accident. It was anger. It was resentment. It was him choosing destruction over accountability.

The story behind that crash had layers. Monte had just been dumped by his girlfriend. But instead of facing the truth about what led to the breakup, he turned his fury toward me. He believed I had something to do with her leaving him, but I didn't. What really happened was far worse than anything I could have done.

His girlfriend left because she found out Monte had drained the oil out of her brand-new car. The engine locked, the damage was irreversible, and she was devastated. She loved that car. She had worked hard for it. When she realized he was behind it, she walked away from him for good.

Rather than take responsibility, Monte redirected the blame toward me. He convinced himself that my girlfriend had something to do with his breakup, that I must have encouraged her to leave him. In his mind, everything bad that happened in his life had to be linked to me. He couldn't process the idea that his own actions were the reason people walked away.

So instead of apologizing or seeking help, Monte snapped. He drove his Maxima full speed into the side of my Mercedes while it was parked. That car wasn't just a vehicle. It represented my progress, my hard work, and my elevation. It was something he couldn't stand to see. Crashing into it was his way of trying to erase my success, even if only symbolically.

But what he didn't realize was this. You can damage my property, but you can't touch my purpose. I replaced the car. What I didn't replace was my tolerance for his behavior. That crash was the final warning sign. It was the moment I realized I had to protect myself from a man who had the same face as me, but a completely different heart.

Monte's spiral didn't stop there. He began lashing out at everyone. Friends. Family. Even strangers online. He made vague threats. Posted cryptic rants. Filed false police reports. He told people I was violent. That I was unstable. That I was a danger. But the only person who had ever demonstrated reckless behavior was him.

I tried to be patient. I tried to be spiritual. I reminded myself of our childhood, of the moments we laughed, of the times we fought side by side. But those memories were now tainted by a man who had lost his grip on reality.

Monte didn't want help. He wanted chaos. He wanted me to lose everything the way he had. But the difference was, I never sabotaged my own blessings. I honored the people in my life. I took responsibility when I failed. And when I stumbled, I got back up with grace.

The crash wasn't just about metal and glass. It was about a soul that had hit rock bottom and refused to ask for help. It was about a man who had burned every bridge and then blamed the river for being too wide to cross.

This chapter is not about a car. It's about a breaking point. The day I chose peace over pain. The moment I decided that love without boundaries is not love—it's bondage.

From that point forward, I stopped making excuses. I stopped trying to rescue him. I stopped allowing his dysfunction to invade my progress. I didn't stop loving Monte. I just stopped enabling him.

Because when someone chooses destruction over growth, the most loving thing you can do is let them face the consequences alone.

# Chapter 11

## The Women Who Tried to Love Him

"Love is patient, love is kind. It does not envy, it does not boast, it is not proud. It does not dishonor others. It is not self-seeking. It is not easily angered. It keeps no record of wrongs." – 1 Corinthians 13:4–5 (NIV)

Some women didn't just date Monte. They survived him.

From the outside, he came off charming. He quoted scripture. He prayed out loud. He wore respectability like a uniform. But behind closed doors, a different man emerged. One who weaponized love, manipulated emotions, and used his pain to punish people who only wanted to love him.

Mary was the first one to tell me something wasn't right. She was elegant, nurturing, and full of wisdom. She truly believed she could help Monte heal. Instead, she became a victim of his paranoia. In a chilling display of emotional violence, Monte accused her of something unimaginable. He claimed she was having an inappropriate relationship with her own son. Not only did he tell people—he called her employer and launched a workplace investigation. She was mortified. Her name was dragged through the mud because of a man she had once prayed with.

Then came Joni. She tried to leave quietly, respectfully, after realizing Monte's anger was escalating. But Monte doesn't let people go. He retaliates. He waited until she was away from her car and drained the oil, knowing the engine would lock. She lost her vehicle, her independence, and a piece of her peace. For Monte, it was never about reconciliation. It was about control.

Sherria had her entire life turned upside down. She had built a career and a reputation. But when Monte realized he couldn't manipulate her anymore, he made one phone call that changed everything. He accused her of performing sexual acts on her underage son. No one saw it coming. Her job launched an investigation. Her name was whispered in hallways. She didn't just cry. She broke. That kind of accusation can destroy a person. And for Monte, it was just another way to get revenge.

But the darkest of them all was the woman from Oklahoma. She was his fiancée. She believed in him. She moved across states to build a life with him. And her only mistake was wearing a sundress. Monte told her she was disrespectful. That she embarrassed him. What followed was a nightmare. He held a gun to her head. He choked her. He screamed at her as if she were his enemy. And when he went to shower, she ran. She didn't even stop to pack. She escaped barefoot and terrified. She later posted on social media, pleading for help to get home. That message wasn't just a cry for help—it was a survival story.

After every woman left, Monte told the same lies. He said they were unstable. He said they were jealous of him. He said they were dangerous. But the truth always echoed louder than his stories.

Each woman thought she could be the one to bring him peace. But Monte was not searching for peace. He was hunting for power. He used affection like bait. He studied their kindness, then turned it against them.

What disturbed me most wasn't just what he did to them. It was how quickly he moved on. No remorse. No reflection. Just a new narrative to fit his ego.

Some of these women reached out to me. Some with tears. Some with questions. Some just wanting to be believed. I told every one of them, you are not crazy. You are not weak. You were not the problem. You simply crossed paths with a man who refuses to face the pain inside him, so he tries to transfer it into others.

Monte used God's name while doing the devil's work. He cloaked abuse in scripture. He disguised dysfunction as love. And when exposed, he cried victim.

This chapter is not just about what he did. It is about what these women survived. And what they walked away from.

To the women who tried to love him, your courage matters. Your voice matters. Your healing matters. You are not a footnote in Monte's delusions. You are evidence that God rescues, protects, and delivers.

You didn't walk away. You escaped. And that escape was the beginning of your freedom.

# Chapter 12

## When Enough Is Enough

"Deliver me from my enemies, O God. Be my fortress against those who are attacking me." – Psalm 59:1 (NIV)

There is only so much a man can take. You can pray. You can forgive. You can hope they change. But when someone keeps crossing the line, over and over again, there comes a moment when you must say, enough is enough. That moment came after years of Monte's false accusations, stalking behavior, and coordinated attacks to destroy my name.

For decades, Monte had been on a mission to sabotage my progress. He inserted himself into court cases, called my jobs, and even showed up where he wasn't welcome. But the situation reached a boiling point in 2024 when he crossed the final line.

After years of disrespecting our mother, yelling at her, cursing at her, and blaming her for his failures, I had finally told him he was no longer welcome in my life. He was not allowed at my house, my job, or any event that I hosted. I meant it, and for a while, I thought he got the message.

But Monte doesn't let go easily. A few days after our last conversation, he sent the police to my house for a wellness check. He claimed I had made threats against him. He knew what he was doing. He wanted to create a paper trail. He wanted to paint me as unstable, hoping the system would respond before the truth caught up to his lies.

What he didn't expect was that I had a witness. The police chief of my town was standing right beside me when the call came in. That chief, a respected official, personally vouched for my behavior and confirmed that Monte's claims were false. When Monte realized his plan had failed, he dropped the charges quietly. But the damage had already been attempted.

That wasn't the only attack. He went further. I had already filed a restraining order against him, and the court approved it. We both agreed to stay away from each other, legally. I gave my jobs copies of the court order. I was serious about protecting my peace.

But the very next evening, on my day off, Monte showed up at my job. I was the head of security at a major venue. When I saw him, I didn't get emotional. I got professional. I followed protocol and placed him on the banned list. He had no business being there, and his presence violated the court's boundaries.

Monte didn't stop. On June 18, 2024, he called the police again, this time to my job. He falsely claimed that I was threatening patrons with a firearm and that I was a felon in multiple states. The goal was clear. He wanted me arrested. He wanted to see me lose everything. But he failed, again.

The truth is, the felony charge he referenced came from an open Florida case that Monte himself instigated. A case that is still under federal appeal. Under the law, I am not a felon because no conviction is final during an open appeal. I am still protected under the Law Enforcement Officers Safety Act. I carry myself with integrity. I work within the law. And I had every legal document to prove it.

Monte has tried everything to bring me down. He has lied to police, called agencies, filed false claims, and embarrassed our family. But the more he attacks, the stronger I stand. Because I am not built on lies. I am built on truth. My foundation is not fear. It is faith.

This chapter is titled When Enough Is Enough because it marks the point where I decided to live free from the emotional leash of a twin who refused to heal. Monte has shown the world who he is. I no longer feel obligated to defend him, protect him, or remain silent for his sake.

I am no longer entertaining the lie. I am walking fully in the light.

This is not revenge. This is release. And as I write these words, I am not angry. I am free.

# Chapter 13

## Peace in the Presence of Madness

"You will keep him in perfect peace, whose mind is stayed on You, because he trusts in You." – Isaiah 26:3 (NKJV)

The hardest part of this journey has never been the lies or the betrayal. It has been keeping my peace when everything in me wanted to react. When your character is attacked, when your name is dragged through the mud, when the very person who shares your DNA tries to rewrite your story with fiction and poison, silence can feel like weakness. But in truth, silence can also be the loudest form of strength.

Monte has tried to provoke me in every way imaginable. He called my jobs. He showed up at places I told him to stay away from. He filed false accusations. He made fake articles. He even tried to convince others that I was mentally unstable. But the one thing he never expected was that I would not break.

People often ask how I remained calm. How I continued to walk in purpose while being harassed by the person who should have been my greatest ally. The answer is simple. God. I knew I was in a spiritual battle. This was not just about Monte. It was about legacy. About identity. About warfare that had existed long before either of us took our first breath.

Monte was battling more than me. He was battling himself. And though I became the target, I was not the enemy. His rage came from the mirror, not from my actions. He hated seeing in me what he had failed to activate in himself.

At times, I felt like I was walking through fire. I would be at work, smiling and leading people, all while knowing that my own brother had just filed something against me behind closed doors. I would hear rumors started by him, designed to assassinate my name. And I had to choose, over and over again, not to retaliate.

I could have fought fire with fire. I could have embarrassed him publicly. I had evidence. I had documents. I had people who were willing to speak on my behalf. But I chose dignity. Not because I was afraid, but because I knew what I carried was too valuable to be wasted on pettiness.

There is power in restraint. It takes discipline to keep your hands clean when someone else keeps throwing mud. But I have learned that peace is more powerful than revenge. And when God is your defender, your enemies will eventually expose themselves.

Monte thought his noise would drown out my truth. But truth is eternal. It does not fade. It does not bend. It does not flinch when threatened. I stood firm because I knew my purpose. I knew my truth. And I knew my God.

This chapter is not just about what Monte did. It is about what I refused to become. I refused to become bitter. I refused to become broken. I refused to let his chaos destroy my calm. I kept my mind focused. I kept my heart guarded. And I kept my eyes on the bigger picture.

Peace is not found in silence alone. It is found in trust. I trusted that my story would speak for itself. I trusted that the right people would see through the lies. And I trusted that God would vindicate me in time.

He did. And He continues to.

Monte tried to create storms. I chose to become the calm. And in doing so, I discovered that peace is not the absence of pain. It is the decision to not let pain control your path.

# Chapter 14

## Running from Himself

"The wise in heart accept commands, but a chattering fool comes to ruin." – Proverbs 10:8 (NIV)

There was a reason Monte changed his last name. He told people it was because someone stole his identity, but that was a lie to cover up a deeper truth. He wasn't running from theft. He was running from himself. Monte had reached a point where he hated everything about the man in the mirror. He hated our last name. He hated his reflection. And most of all, he hated that no matter how hard he tried, he could not outgrow his own failures.

The truth is, Monte didn't change his name because of me. He changed it because he could not face the life he had created. A life built on deception, failure, and missed opportunities. He thought a new name would give him a new beginning. But the problem wasn't the name. The problem was the man behind it.

He filed bankruptcy multiple times in multiple states. In both Pennsylvania and California, his financial wreckage was public record. He didn't lose it all once. He lost it repeatedly. And instead of taking accountability, he spun the narrative. He blamed others. He acted like a victim. But the court documents said otherwise.

Monte also had legal charges on his record. In one case, he was charged with simple assault. In another, he faced allegations of sexual harassment. These weren't minor rumors. These were real cases with real consequences. But in Monte's world, nothing was ever his fault. Every bad decision had a scapegoat.

What made it worse was that Monte constantly tried to compete with me in areas where he had no foundation. He would flash pictures from my life, pretend they were his, and introduce himself to people as a decorated man of influence. But behind closed doors, he was unstable. He used the language of success, but never lived the discipline required to achieve it.

Monte became an Elder because of me. He failed the test repeatedly. I sat with him and gave him the answers. I stood up in church and made the motion that no one else was willing to make. And when he finally got the title, he threw it in my face like he had earned it all on his own.

He won first place in martial arts tournaments because I was the judge. If I hadn't been there, he would have never placed. I coached him. I corrected his form. I gave him the advantage that other competitors never had. And instead of thanking me, he used those trophies as weapons to claim superiority.

Monte was introduced to the luxury lifestyle through me. When I bought my first Rolls Royce, he bragged to everyone as if it were his. He took photos, sent them to people, and told them that he had reached the top. But the truth was, he never put in the work. He just stood beside me long enough to get the picture.

There is a dangerous kind of pride that feeds off another person's shine. Monte didn't want to be successful. He wanted to look successful. And when the image cracked, he changed his name to hide the pieces.

But names don't fix broken spirits. They don't erase court records. They don't delete betrayal. And they certainly don't silence truth.

This chapter is about accountability. Monte has spent his entire adult life dodging it. But no matter how many aliases he uses, the truth still knows his address. I didn't write this to shame him. I wrote it to show that running from yourself only leads to exhaustion. You can't reinvent a future if you're not willing to face your past.

Monte didn't fail because of me. He failed because he refused to be real. And while he kept trying to rewrite the narrative, I kept building mine on facts, faith, and the kind of hard work he never respected.

In the end, he didn't run from the Burno name. He ran from the burden of carrying truth.

# Chapter 15

## The Fabricator

"A false witness will not go unpunished, and whoever pours out lies will perish." – Proverbs 19:9 (NIV)

Monte has spent much of his life trying to rewrite history. Not just the past, but his place in it. He does not just lie to others. He lies to himself. He reinvents facts, inflates his achievements, and inserts himself into moments he never earned. In his mind, being associated with greatness is just as good as being great. But association without work is delusion.

One of the earliest examples came during our time in the military. Monte and I joined together under the Buddy System. But from the very beginning, it was clear he was not built for it. While I took the challenges seriously and adapted to the structure, Monte struggled with everything—especially physical training. He could not complete the required drills. He lagged behind on the runs. He even used the road guard position to rest while the rest of us kept pushing forward.

I remember one morning when we had a critical fitness test. Monte was already falling behind, and if he didn't pass, he would be recycled or sent home. Myself and another soldier, Jonathan Hickman, literally ran beside him, motivating him every step of the way. We shouted words of encouragement. We kept pace with him. We didn't let him fall. And somehow, through our support, he made it through that run. At the end of it, Monte collapsed in tears. He shouted praise, cried out to God, and told the drill sergeants he was grateful for our help.

The drill sergeants pulled me aside later and said, "Burno, if you hadn't pushed your brother, he would have been on the first bus out of here." That moment could have been Monte's turning point. It could have sparked humility. But instead, it became another memory he distorted. He began telling people he breezed through training, that he was top of the class. The truth was, he was on the edge of discharge, and only got through it because others carried him.

After barely making it through those early weeks, Monte still ended up being removed from service. The Army cited his inability to adapt to military life and noted mental instability, including suicidal tendencies. His separation was not honorable. It was administrative and necessary.

And yet, to this day, he speaks about his military experience as if it were a badge of honor. He wears camouflage clothing and references his time in service like he earned a medal. But real soldiers know the truth. He couldn't handle the discipline. He couldn't handle the structure. And he couldn't handle the reality that he wasn't cut out for it.

This pattern followed him into every area of life. He lied about his roles in law enforcement, claiming he was a high-ranking official. He inflated his position with the Guardian Angels, calling himself a Lieutenant Commander, a title that didn't even exist in our structure. He exaggerated his martial arts background, skipped the discipline, and bragged about tournaments he only won because I was the one judging.

When I began producing films, managing artists, and building a career rooted in real achievement, Monte clung to my name like a lifeline. He told people he was a partner in my success. He said he co-created my businesses. He even claimed he was instrumental in forming my connections. But there was no paperwork. No contracts. No real involvement. Just proximity and a mouth full of fiction.

Monte also created false headlines to fuel his illusions. One of the worst was a fake article claiming I had stolen his identity. It was complete fabrication, written by him, with no credible source, but designed to look official. He circulated it online, hoping it would stick. It didn't.

What Monte never realized is that pretending does not protect you from the truth. You can change your name, your story, and your image, but you cannot escape what you refuse to confront. The fabrications might fool the uninformed, but they crumble under the weight of reality.

This chapter is not written to embarrass Monte. It is written to expose the cost of falsehood. Monte could have had his own journey. He could have built something meaningful. But he chose to borrow instead of build. To lie instead of learn. And when things didn't go his way, he blamed me for standing in a spotlight he never earned.

I carried him in basic training, just like I tried to carry him in life. But at some point, you have to let go of those who refuse to walk on their own.

# Chapter 16

## Receipts Never Lie

"Let another praise you, and not your own mouth; a stranger, and not your own lips." – Proverbs 27:2 (ESV)

In a world full of lies, there is one thing that always speaks louder than opinion—receipts. Not just the kind printed on paper, but the kind earned through years of work, credibility, and sacrifice. I do not have to speak for myself. My resume does that. My affiliations, my awards, my titles, and my life's work stand tall without me saying a word. Monte, on the other hand, has spent his life trying to erase those receipts because he could never produce any of his own.

Let the truth be clear. I have served in law enforcement. I earned my state certification. I passed every investigation and completed a fast-track program designed for elite candidates. I served as the Executive Director for the Alliance of the Guardian Angels under the direct leadership of Curtis Sliwa. I am a member of the Screen Actors Guild, the American Federation of Television and Radio Artists, and the National Fraternal Order of Police.

I am a registered member of ASCAP, the American Society of Composers, Authors, and Publishers. I am a certified member of the United Martial Arts Referee Association. I am also a proud member of the Most Worshipful Prince Hall Grand Lodge, a historic and respected branch of the Masonic order that honors brotherhood, service, and integrity.

I have IMDB credits as a producer. I have managed and protected Grammy-winning,

Emmy-winning, and platinum-selling artists both nationally and across the globe. My work in the entertainment industry speaks for itself. From managing international tours to coordinating elite-level security for high-profile talent, I have earned the respect of professionals across the world.

I hold black belts in multiple martial arts disciplines and opened my own martial arts academy. I do not say this to boast. I say it because every step was earned, not imagined. Every line on my resume can be verified. Monte cannot stand that.

He has gone so far as to tell people that I forged my law enforcement credentials. That my affiliations are fake. That my title with the Guardian Angels was made up. He even accused me of lying about my involvement in the entertainment industry. But none of those lies could ever match the weight of documented truth. When background checks are run, my name passes.
When certifications are checked, mine appear. When people call for references, doors open.

Monte, meanwhile, has no track record—only stories. He has told people that celebrities gave him luxury cars. That he was involved in films that never existed. That he co-founded organizations he was never invited to. And when questioned, he gets defensive. He lashes out, claiming I am the one who lies. But where are his receipts? Where are his titles? His memberships? His credentials?

This chapter is not about bragging. It is about drawing a line between what is real and what is made up. Monte does not just compete with me. He tries to undo my truth by discrediting the very things I worked for. He does it because seeing my progress reminds him of his own lack of growth. But envy does not erase evidence.

When I earned my Florida Law Enforcement Certification, both

Osceola County and Orange County expressed interest in hiring me. But Monte acted on the racially corrupt history of law enforcement in Lake County, Florida—a legacy so notorious that it has been publicly exposed on CNN and ABC News. He exploited that bias by writing an anonymous letter to the Florida Department of Law Enforcement, pretending to be a church bishop. He made false claims against me with the hope of blocking my opportunities. And sadly, despite my qualifications, his actions contributed to the delay of my career advancement.

This injustice has not gone unanswered. I currently have an open case in Federal court to resolve this matter. I have faith in the legal process and confidence that the truth will prevail.

Monte is not just threatened by my success. He is tormented by it. And instead of doing the work, he chooses to attack from the sidelines. But you cannot assassinate character that has already stood through the storm.

I do not need to respond to every lie. I just continue to live my truth. And truth has a funny way of rising when the noise fades.

This chapter is for anyone who has ever had their success questioned by someone too lazy to create their own. Let your work speak. Let your life speak. Let your consistency destroy the narrative.

Monte made it his mission to tear down everything I built. But what he failed to understand is that what God has established, no man can dismantle.

# Chapter 17

## From Pain to Purpose: The Truth About Healing

"The Lord is close to the brokenhearted and saves those who are crushed in spirit." – Psalm 34:18 (NIV)

Healing is not a straight line. It is not a soft whisper or a gentle breeze. Sometimes it feels like war, especially when the person you need healing from shares your blood, your face, and your last name.

I grew up believing what many of us were taught: "What goes on in this house, stays in this house." But keeping quiet does not stop the pain. It preserves it. And for years, that pain turned into pressure. Pressure to protect. Pressure to pretend. Pressure to survive.

Monte was not just my twin. He was supposed to be my other half. But as we grew older, I watched him become a stranger. He carried secrets in his eyes and anger in his chest. The world saw the polite version of him, but I saw the man who sabotaged relationships, spread lies, and tried to destroy everything I built just so he could feel powerful.

What no one talks about enough is how mental illness in the family can tear apart foundations that look solid on the outside. Monte was diagnosed by a U.S. Army psychiatrist with mental instability, including Sibling Jealousy Syndrome. He was discharged just 28 days into basic training for failing to adapt. The same military journey I completed with discipline and honor broke him almost immediately. While I pushed through obstacle courses, Monte cried in corners. I encouraged him. Another soldier, Jonathan Hickman, and I did everything we could to lift him up. But Monte did not want help. He wanted control.

He came into my world not as a supporter, but as a saboteur. When I managed and protected Grammy-winning, Emmy-winning, and platinum-selling artists, he spread rumors to make it look like I was the imposter. When I launched businesses and appeared in films with real IMDb credits, he called people claiming I was living a lie while fabricating his own stories about Jay-Z and Beyoncé buying him a Rolls Royce.

But you cannot bury purpose under bitterness. And you cannot erase favor with falsehood.

The deeper truth is that Monte does not hate me because of who I am. He hates me because of who he is not. My success highlights his stagnation. My healing exposes his dysfunction. My peace disturbs his chaos.

What took me years to understand is that mental illness wears many masks. In Monte, it wore the mask of arrogance. It wore the mask of religiosity. It wore the mask of "I am the victim." But underneath was a broken man who never got the help he needed. And as much as I prayed, hoped, and extended grace, he chose to weaponize his pain instead of treat it.

That choice cost him everything.

It cost him his family. It cost him my trust. And eventually, it cost him access to my life.

But here is the part most people do not understand. I still love my brother. I do not carry hate in my heart. What I carry is wisdom. The wisdom to know that love is not a license for someone to abuse you. The wisdom to know that boundaries are not betrayal. They are survival.

Healing required me to face hard truths. That no apology may ever come. That the person who hurt me may never change. That my peace may offend people who benefited from my silence. And I had to be okay with that.

I want this chapter to speak to every reader who has suffered silently. Every son, daughter, sibling, or spouse who was told to keep quiet. Every person whose abuser hides behind prayer, family ties, or fake humility. You deserve to heal. You deserve to tell the truth. You deserve to be free.

Pain was not the end of my story. It was the beginning of my purpose. I now speak for those who cannot speak for themselves. I now build what I wish I had. I now tell the truth not to shame Monte, but to set someone else free from their own silence.

This book is more than a memoir. It is a movement.

Let this be the moment you choose healing. Let this be the moment you say, "No more." Let this be the chapter that shows you that pain does not have to be permanent, and family does not have to be fatal.

Healing is holy. Truth is powerful. And purpose is born in the fire.

# Chapter 18

## The Strength to Forgive

"Be kind to one another, tenderhearted, forgiving one another, as God in Christ forgave you." – Ephesians 4:32 (ESV)

I used to think forgiveness meant forgetting. I thought it meant letting people off the hook, especially when they never said sorry. But the older I got, the more I realized forgiveness is not weakness. It is strength. Forgiveness does not excuse what someone did. It simply refuses to let their actions control your future.

Forgiving Monte was one of the hardest things I ever had to do. Not because he asked for it, but because I needed peace. Monte never gave me closure. He never took accountability. He never acknowledged the damage he caused. Instead, he acted like nothing happened. Or worse, he acted like it was all my fault.

I spent years holding on to the pain, replaying the lies, the sabotage, the betrayal. I carried the weight of every false report he filed, every rumor he spread, every relationship he ruined. I thought holding onto the anger would protect me, but it only poisoned me. I was surviving, but I was not free.

Forgiveness is not about letting someone back into your life. It is about releasing the grip they have on your heart. It is about breaking the cycle of resentment so your soul can breathe again. When I forgave Monte, it was not for him. It was for me. I had to make peace with the fact that some people will never see the pain they caused. They will never apologize. They will never change. And that is okay. My healing cannot wait for someone else's apology.

I do not forgive to forget. I forgive to heal.

There were days I cried, not because I missed him, but because I could not understand how someone I loved could hate me so deeply. There were nights I asked God why my own brother would work so hard to destroy me. The answer was not in the why, but in the who I was becoming. Every betrayal made me stronger. Every lie taught me truth. Every heartbreak built my resilience.

Monte's behavior revealed his condition, not my worth.

I learned that you can love someone and still protect your peace. You can pray for someone and still keep your distance. You can wish them well and still walk away. That is maturity. That is freedom.

Forgiveness did not mean I stopped telling the truth. It meant I stopped being consumed by the lie. I can tell my story without bitterness. I can speak his name without rage. I can recall the events without shaking. That is healing.

Some people may not understand why I still say I love my brother after all he has done. But love does not always look like closeness. Sometimes, love is setting a boundary so you both can grow. Sometimes, love is praying for someone from afar. Sometimes, love is telling your truth so the silence does not kill you.

I forgave Monte, not because he deserved it, but because I deserved peace.

To anyone reading this who has been hurt by a family member, I want you to know that you are not alone. You are not weak for hurting. You are not wrong for walking away. And you are not broken beyond repair. Healing is your birthright. Peace is your inheritance. Forgiveness is your power.

Forgiveness is not the end of the story. It is the beginning of a new one.

# Chapter 19

## The Broken Mirror

"For now we see in a mirror dimly, but then face to face." – 1 Corinthians 13:12 (ESV)

Looking at Monte was like looking into a cracked mirror. We share the same face, the same birthday, the same blood. But what stared back at me was not my reflection. It was a fractured version of what could have been.

Monte always walked with a chip on his shoulder. He did not just want to be seen. He wanted to be seen as better than me. If I succeeded, he questioned how. If I failed, he cheered quietly. If I cried, he called me weak. If I stood strong, he called me arrogant. It was not rivalry. It was resentment.

Growing up, we were close. But somewhere along the line, the mirror cracked. I started chasing purpose. He started chasing power. I started building. He started destroying. And I could not figure out why. It took time and painful experiences to learn that some people will always compare themselves to you, no matter how much love you offer. Especially when your wins remind them of what they lost in themselves.

Monte tried to reflect my life as his own. He told people my car was his. My house was his. My awards were his. He even posed in my clothes. When I saw the photos, I was not angry. I was sad. Sad that he had to live in my shadow just to feel light. Sad that he could not recognize his own value without stealing mine.

He did not need to become me. He needed to find himself.

But Monte never wanted reflection. He wanted recognition. He wanted credit without the work. He wanted the image without the integrity. He wanted the spotlight without the sacrifice.

The mirror did not lie. But it revealed what he refused to face.

And here's the truth: the mirror does two things. It allows us to fix what we see, and it allows us to reflect what we see. Monte refused both. He never tried to correct what was broken within. Instead, he performed for approval, reflected lies, and ignored every opportunity to confront himself.

He told people I abandoned him, but he left himself a long time ago. He accused me of sabotage, but he had been sabotaging his own life for years. Failed jobs, failed relationships, failed trust. All the while pointing fingers instead of taking ownership.

I remember one night clearly. I was on my knees praying, not for success, not for revenge, but for understanding. I asked God, "How do you love someone who keeps cutting you?" The answer came quietly: "You love them from a healed place, not a hurting one."

From that day on, I stopped trying to fix the mirror. Some things cannot be repaired. They have to be replaced. I replaced hope in Monte with hope in myself. I replaced wishing for his change with working on mine. I replaced trying to be understood with accepting that I may never be.

The mirror between us remains cracked. But I am no longer trying to make it whole. I am whole.

What I see now is not a twin, but a warning. A reminder of what happens when you live through ego instead of truth. A reminder of why healing matters. A reminder of how far I have come.

Monte still uses my name to get in doors he cannot open on his own. He still tells stories that only he believes. But I no longer react. I no longer defend what is already proven. I let the truth be my voice, and my peace be my proof.

If you have someone in your life who mirrors you but hates you, understand this: you are not the problem. Their reflection is. You are a light they cannot dim, a truth they cannot duplicate. And no matter how many times they try to distort the image, your worth remains intact.

The mirror is broken. But I am not.

# Chapter 20

## When Ego Turns Dangerous

"Pride goes before destruction, and a haughty spirit before a fall." – Proverbs 16:18 (ESV)

S ome people are not destroyed by their enemies. They are destroyed by their ego. Monte was one of those people.

Over the years, I have watched him go from insecure to unstable, from jealous to reckless. But nothing prepared me for the moment I learned he was plotting to have our own father killed. It was not some heated argument or emotional outburst. It was calculated. Cold. And absolutely unforgivable.

It started with a conversation that should have never happened. My cousin called me, shaken. He said Monte had offered him half the money from our father's lockbox in exchange for his life. I was stunned. My cousin repeated it. Monte told him, "I know where he keeps it. If we do this right, no one will suspect a thing."

What kind of man arranges to have his father murdered over money? What kind of heart carries that much hatred for the man who gave him life? Our father was not perfect, but he was present. He tried to help us. He loved us. And Monte, out of resentment and entitlement, viewed him as an obstacle instead of a father. That is when I realized Monte's issue was not just with me. It was with anything or anyone that challenged his sense of control.

I confronted my cousin again to be sure, and then we involved our father on a three-way call. I will never forget the sound of silence on the other end when my cousin repeated the offer out loud. Monte did not deny it. He did not cry. He did not even explain. He just sat with the weight of what he had done, as if it were normal. That was the moment I knew. Something in him was broken beyond reason.

Years later, I would see that same pride and delusion rear its head in a different setting. This time, it was during our martial arts training.

Monte and I were both studying under SiFu Rome, a master who commanded respect. We were learning traditional Hung Gar Kung Fu. I had been chosen many times to lead the class in SiFu's absence because of my discipline and precision. Monte hated that. He saw it as favoritism rather than earned trust. One day, in front of the entire class, Monte challenged SiFu Rome.

It was a dangerous move. Not physically, but culturally and spiritually. In martial arts, you do not challenge your teacher unless you are ready to face the consequences. But Monte, in his usual prideful fashion, wanted to prove something.

SiFu Rome responded with the wisdom of a true master. He did not strike Monte. Instead, he ordered the entire class to line up and begin intense bone conditioning exercises. Hours passed. Sweat poured. Students dropped to their knees from exhaustion. Monte began to cry, not because of pain, but from the realization of what he had done. He was not facing just physical resistance. He was facing spiritual discipline.

When the final stance was done, SiFu Rome called the class to attention. He looked Monte in the eye and said, "I did this because I love you. Anyone else, I would have destroyed." Then he added something deeper. "To challenge your teacher is to challenge your own growth."

Monte never fully recovered from that embarrassment. He continued training for a while, even competing in tournaments. But the shame of being corrected publicly by a man he once tried to impress burned into his pride.

He never saw correction as love. He saw it as competition. That is why he continued down a path of sabotage and self-destruction. He believed life was about domination, not discipline. About winning, not wisdom.

But ego has a short fuse. And when it explodes, it destroys everything in its path, including family.

I tell these stories not out of bitterness, but out of clarity. I want the reader to understand how dangerous pride can become when it festers unchecked. Monte is not just my brother. He is a warning. A living example of what happens when you let envy poison your soul.

I pray for him still. But I also protect myself from him. Because sometimes, love means setting a boundary so the broken cannot break you too.

This chapter is not just about Monte. It is about how unchecked pride can lead people to do unthinkable things. It is about recognizing the signs, speaking the truth, and never letting someone else's ego rewrite your legacy.

I have chosen peace. I have chosen truth. I have chosen to expose the darkness, not to shame, but to set the record straight.

Because when ego turns dangerous, silence is no longer safety. It is surrender.

# Chapter 21

## A Stranger in My Shoes

"Nothing is hidden that will not be made manifest, nor is anything secret that will not be known and come to light." – Luke 8:17 (ESV)

What do you call someone who wants your life but does not want your struggle? Someone who does not build, but steals. Someone who does not admire, but imitates. The word is imposter. And Monte wore that role better than any title he ever claimed.

I had taken a trip to Las Vegas to handle business and relax for a few days. While I was gone, Monte made a decision that stunned everyone involved. He flew in a woman named Tiffany from Detroit, a woman he had been speaking to for a while, and used that time to craft one of the most bizarre and disrespectful lies he ever told.

He welcomed Tiffany into my home — not as a guest, but as the supposed owner. He gave her a tour, pointing to my plaques and awards, claiming they were his. He even told her that the house was his, the car outside was his, and that he was the man who built this successful life. It was a performance worthy of an award. But this time, his audience would wake up.

Monte drove my vehicle, my car that I had worked hard for and parked in my driveway before leaving town. He picked up my daughter and mother and took them all to the market as if he were head of the household. While driving, he kept the act going. Talking with our mother, he continued selling his version of reality.

Then he crossed a line that left everyone in the car uncomfortable. Monte told Tiffany that I was not a real person. He claimed he had to send my plaques back to the manufacturer because they had the wrong name on them. He insisted that everything she saw belonged to him and that I was just a character he created. In that moment, he did not just lie about me — he tried to erase me.

But he did not count on my daughter speaking up.

"That's my dad's things," she said, her voice clear and confident. A child's truth in the middle of a grown man's lie.

Our mother quickly interrupted, telling my daughter to be quiet and stay out of grown folks' conversations.

"But Grandma," my daughter replied, her voice cracking with confusion. Even she could feel the injustice in what was happening.

A week later, I returned home early. I walked into the house and before I could say a word, my daughter ran toward me and jumped into my arms. Her eyes lit up as she looked at Tiffany and said, "I told you my dad was real!"

Tiffany looked like she had seen a ghost. Her face went pale. Her mouth opened, but no words came out at first. After a moment, she said, "Oh my God. I have something to tell you."

Monte, clearly panicked, began rushing her to grab her things. He wanted her gone before the truth could fully surface. He tried to pack her up, get her out the door, and silence her before she could speak. But it was too late.

I gave her my business card before she left. When she returned to Detroit, she called me. She explained everything. She told me how

Monte had lied, used her, and manipulated the entire situation. Her voice trembled with emotion. She said she felt tricked and humiliated. And then she said something that broke my heart and gave me peace at the same time.

"I feel like I was dating a ghost, but you were the real person. He's just a shadow."

That moment confirmed everything. Monte did not want a relationship. He wanted a role. He wanted to be me without paying the price to become himself.

My mother later told me she never gave Monte permission to be in the house or drive my car without her present. She had trusted him, assumed he had changed, and was devastated by the truth. She promised me that it would never happen again.

This chapter is not just about a woman or a lie. It is about how far someone will go when they have no identity of their own. Monte did not just want a piece of my life. He wanted to wear my skin, walk in my shoes, and live in my accomplishments. But impersonation will never be equal to authenticity.

No matter how many people he fools, the truth always shows up. In this case, it showed up as a little girl telling the truth in front of a grown man's lie. And that truth exposed everything.

# Chapter 22

## Women He Couldn't Have, So He Tried to Steal Mine

"The thief comes only to steal and kill and destroy; I came that they may have life, and have it abundantly." — John 10:10 (NASB)

When a man is so deeply broken inside that he seeks validation through deception, he becomes a threat not only to others but to himself. Monte became that kind of man. His insecurities ran so deep, he tried to compete with me through women I was dating. It didn't matter if I was happy or if the relationship was meaningful. If he saw light shining on me, he tried to dim it by inserting himself into my personal life.

One of the first signs of his sickness showed up on my 21st birthday. My girlfriend at the time, Connie, came to my party. We had just had a disagreement, so our vibe that night was a little off. We were cordial, but not affectionate. Connie was striking. She wore a red mini skirt, black fishnet stockings, red fingernails, red lipstick, and her long hair flowing down her back. She walked in looking like a cover model. Monte noticed it. He also noticed the slight tension between us and wasted no time being inappropriate. He leaned over to her and said, "If you and Lamar are done with each other, I'll gladly take you and hold you."

Connie later told me that moment made her incredibly uncomfortable. She left the party early and never told me why until years later. She said she didn't want to cause problems between me and my brother, but she had never felt so disrespected by someone who was supposed to be family.

That was just one example. Monte had a pattern. He couldn't build his own happiness, so he targeted mine. Another time, Monte tried to seduce a mutual friend I had confided in. What he didn't know was that this woman had a strong sense of identity, integrity, and discernment. She shared with me exactly how he operated, in her own words:

"Thank u kindly 4being who u r. I'm the same way & in my youth would've gladly accepted ur 'challenge' (have yet 2have anyone since losing my innocence @17 'rock my world' - Lol!) but I'm 2 'seasoned' 2play those games anymore nor do I desire 2... I sent an MMS pic msg (sexually humorous) as I often do w/my friends that are mature enuf 2handle that side of me 2show that I'm NOT always 'SUPER SERIOUS & SPIRITUAL' (I call it my 'character balance'). After realizing what he was attempting 2do & that his insistent proclaim 2 being single & wantin 2c what I was made of wasn't workin, I calld him on it..."

She continued:

"Ok, I can see that my brotha has won again but I'm cool w/it besides he really likes u more anyway. I'm praying 4the best btwn u2 'Ms Heartbreaker'!"

He went from aggressive to passive in a matter of moments. When he realized he wasn't going to charm her into giving him her attention, he tried to save face by praising me instead. That message confirmed everything I already knew. Monte viewed every part of my life as a competition, and whenever I found joy, he saw it as a loss for himself.

There were more examples. One evening, Monte, Dee, and I were walking through the park. He tripped us into the grass on purpose, pretending it was a joke, but then began dry humping Dee right in front of me. She was stunned. I was furious. That wasn't a joke. It was another attempt to violate boundaries and embarrass me.

Then came the incident in Pineville, North Carolina. I welcomed Monte into my home while he was visiting. While I was working, he was stirring conflict. He whispered lies and half-truths to my girlfriend, causing unnecessary arguments between us. Eventually, he manipulated her into sleeping with him multiple times in my own home.

There was a woman named Regina. We were spending time together casually, enjoying a connection. Monte saw her once and that was all it took. He filled her head with lies, distorted her view of me, and then slept with her. When he was finished, he discarded her. There was no love in it, only conquest.

The most painful moment was when he interfered in a relationship I believed would lead to marriage. I met a woman online who was elegant, spiritual, and connected to me on every level. Just when our relationship was gaining depth, she disappeared without explanation. I later found out Monte had messaged her pretending to be a concerned friend. He told her I had AIDS and that I was sleeping with women in multiple states. She believed him because he was my twin. She thought she was protecting herself. Monte poisoned what could have been the most meaningful relationship of my life.

He didn't stop there. Monte sent messages to other women I was dating, repeating the same tactics. Lies. Fear. Manipulation. One woman broke down crying when I showed her proof of his deception. She said, "I only believed him because you're twins. I thought twins looked out for each other."

I didn't have a response. Just pain.

Monte's attacks on my relationships weren't about desire. They were about control. He didn't want the women. He wanted to take something from me. He saw my happiness as something he needed to destroy so that he wouldn't have to face the emptiness in his own life.

But here's what Monte failed to understand. My character is not built on the approval of others. My peace comes from God. And while he lurked in the shadows of jealousy, I stood in the light of truth.

To the man reading this, I say this with conviction. Protect your relationships. Pay attention to those closest to you. Not every smile means you well. Sometimes the most dangerous person is the one with your same blood, your same last name, and the same face staring back at you in old photographs.

I don't hate Monte. I see him for what he is. And I forgive him. But I'll never let him near my heart again.

# Chapter 23

## The Cost of Being the Strong One

"Come to Me, all who are weary and burdened, and I will give you rest." — Matthew 11:28 (NASB)

Everyone expects the strong one to never break. You are the protector, the provider, the problem solver. You show up when others fall apart. But no one ever stops to ask, "Who is holding you together?"

For most of my life, I was the strong one. The one who held the line when everything around me was collapsing. When Monte lost control, I stepped in. When family drama erupted, I became the peacemaker. When others lied on me, I did not lash out. I stayed composed. And when I achieved anything, I carried the weight of defending it against jealousy, sabotage, and doubt.

But strength, when not balanced with space to heal, becomes a quiet suffering.

There were days I woke up and did not recognize my own reflection. I looked strong. I spoke with clarity and walked with confidence. But internally, I was carrying trauma stacked on top of betrayal. Not just from Monte, but from years of being the one everybody leaned on, while I had no one to lean on myself.

I have never told anyone this before, but I remember a night, years ago, when I sat in my car outside my house for nearly two hours. I did not go inside. I did not answer my phone. I did not listen to music. I just stared out the windshield. I was not angry. I was not depressed. I was just tired. Not from work, but from the responsibility of being okay all the time.

You do not get to be vulnerable when people see you as unshakable. You do not get to cry when people call you the rock. Even in the church, I was expected to be solid. But what people did not see were the private moments. The prayers I whispered in hotel rooms. The tears I held back when people spoke lies about me publicly. The loneliness that came from knowing that even those closest to me sometimes only saw what I could do, not who I was.

Monte took advantage of that image. He painted me as arrogant, as if I had no flaws, no feelings, no soul. He weaponized the very strength I had spent years developing. But what he never understood is that my strength was not pride. It was survival.

Every scar I carry came from battles I never asked for. I did not choose this fight. I inherited it. I inherited it the moment I chose to break the cycle and speak out. The moment I refused to pretend that everything was okay just to protect an illusion of family unity. The moment I said, "Enough is enough."

Being the strong one cost me relationships. It cost me peace. Sometimes it even cost me sleep. But it never cost me my purpose.

The truth is, I never wanted to be the strong one. I just became what was needed. I stood tall so my family could lean. I carried pain so others would not have to. I took the hits because I knew I could recover.

But I am not ashamed to say it now. I needed someone too.

Someone to see me beyond my accomplishments. Someone to hear me without judgment. Someone to say, "You do not have to be strong today. I have got you." That kind of love is rare. And when you are known more for what you do than who you are, it feels almost unreachable.

But I have found strength in something greater. In God. In prayer. In purpose. And in being able to finally speak the truth without fear.

To the reader who has always had to be the strong one, this chapter is for you. I see you. I understand the silent weight you carry. You are not weak for wanting rest. You are not broken for needing someone. And you are not alone.

Let this be your permission to exhale, to cry, to admit that even the strong get tired. And to remember that your value is not in how much you carry, but in who you are when you finally lay the burden down.

# Chapter 24

## The Warrior Within

"Blessed be the Lord, my rock, who trains my hands for war, and my fingers for battle." — Psalm 144:1 (NASB)

When I was younger, I thought martial arts was about fighting. I saw the power, the speed, the technique, and I wanted it. I wanted the ability to protect myself, to win, to dominate. But as I grew older and more seasoned, I realized something deeper. Martial arts was not just about fighting others. It was about mastering myself.

The discipline of martial arts saved my life. It taught me how to move when I wanted to stand still, how to breathe when my soul was gasping, and how to focus when chaos surrounded me. In many ways, it taught me more than school, church, or the streets ever could. It gave me a code. A compass. A quiet fire inside.

The journey began with learning to defeat an opponent. Man against man. I stood across from people who were trained to hurt me, and I had to learn how to read them, not just their hands, but their eyes. Their spirit. Their energy. Every match was a mental game. It was not about who was stronger. It was about who was smarter, who could control their emotions under pressure, and who could walk away without needing revenge.

Then came the challenge of man against nature. Learning to train in the rain, in the cold, and in uncomfortable spaces. Conditioning my body when it ached, pushing beyond physical limits when my muscles screamed. Martial arts taught me that the world will not always be soft or accommodating. You have to learn how to survive when life is inconvenient, painful, or unkind. That is nature. It is not personal. It simply is.

But the hardest battle of all was man against himself.

Martial arts forced me to confront my pride, my fears, my insecurities, and my anger. There were moments I wanted to quit. Moments I doubted I was good enough. Moments I trained while my heart was broken or my name was being slandered. But I kept going. Not because I had something to prove, but because I had something to become.

I remember days where Monte would watch me train and mock me. He did not understand the silence, the breathing, the bowing, or the hours of repetition. To him, it was either flashy or foolish. He wanted the belt without the bruises, the praise without the pain. And that is why he never truly got it. Martial arts does not reward ego. It rewards humility.

I trained under masters who broke me down to build me up. I was called The Young Tiger by SiFu Rome because of the way I moved, sleek, sharp, and silent. But even tigers must learn patience. I studied the old forms. I respected the lineage. And over time, I became more than just a fighter. I became a warrior in spirit.

Martial arts taught me that there are three enemies every man must defeat before he can truly rise: the man in front of him, the elements around him, and the darkness inside him. Once you conquer all three, there is nothing you cannot achieve.

It gave me the tools to face Monte without raising my fists. It gave me the strength to remain calm when slandered. It gave me clarity when I was lost in emotional fog. And it gave me honor when the world wanted me to seek revenge.

To this day, I carry the spirit of the warrior with me. In business. In relationships. In life. Not to intimidate, but to stand. Not to fight, but to protect. Not to win, but to endure.

To the reader who is fighting battles no one sees, know this. Your greatest opponent is not the one shouting in your face. It is the voice inside that says, "You are not enough." Silence that voice with discipline, with truth, and with faith.

Because when you finally master yourself, you become unstoppable.

# Chapter 25

## From Pain to Power, from Fighter to Father

"You intended to harm me, but God intended it for good, to accomplish what is now being done, the saving of many lives." — Genesis 50:20 (NIV)

There comes a moment in every man's life when he has to stop surviving and start building. I reached that moment after the battles, the betrayals, and the years of being attacked by someone who shared my name and my blood. I was tired of defending my name. I was ready to define it. That is when The Shaolin Experience Academy was born.

It was never just about martial arts. It was about purpose. It was about legacy. I wanted to create something that turned pain into precision, and anger into alignment. I wanted to give others what martial arts had given me: discipline, identity, confidence, and peace. I had seen firsthand how life could tear a man apart, and I knew what it took to be put back together.

So I began to teach. Not just how to block or strike, but how to stand. How to breathe through conflict. How to control the storm within. Every movement I taught had a lesson behind it. Every form had a meaning. The academy was more than a school. It was a sanctuary. A place where people of all ages, from all walks of life, came not just to fight, but to heal.

The Shaolin Creed and Student Oath were not just poetic statements. They were vows of honor. When my students repeated those words, they were not just joining a class. They were joining a code. A way of life rooted in balance, respect, and self-mastery.

74

I poured into my students because I knew what it felt like to be poured out. I had carried so much weight for so long that I wanted to teach others how to fight without becoming bitter, how to defend without destroying, and how to rise without revenge.

Monte thought he was breaking me. What he did not know was that every lie he told, every attempt to sabotage me, every courtroom manipulation, every false report, was sharpening me. He made me better. Not because he wanted to, but because he forced me to choose between falling apart and rising above.

And I chose to rise.

From the outside, it may have looked like I was simply running a martial arts school. But what I was really doing was building warriors. Not street fighters, but spiritual fighters. Not people obsessed with violence, but people committed to discipline, structure, and inner peace. I saw men reconnect with their sons, women reclaim their confidence, and young people who were headed down the wrong path find their footing.

It became clear to me that everything I had gone through had prepared me for this.

The betrayal pushed me to be more compassionate. The pain gave me depth. The public attacks strengthened my faith. And the lies made me appreciate the power of truth. My academy became the place where those lessons were passed down. Every belt, every bow, every bead of sweat on the mat was a testimony.

This was no longer about Monte. This was about mission. I was no longer reacting to what had been done to me. I was building what would outlive me.

To the reader who feels like your suffering has no purpose, let this chapter speak to your heart. Everything you have been through is not the end of your story. It may just be the beginning of your legacy. You are not what they did to you. You are what you choose to do in response.

The world tried to make me a victim. I became a vessel. A vessel for wisdom. A vessel for change. A vessel for generations of warriors who will walk out of my academy carrying more than just technique. They will carry identity. They will carry peace. They will carry purpose.

And that, to me, is victory.

# Chapter 26

## A Legacy Built on Purpose

"A good man leaves an inheritance to his children's children, and the wealth of the sinner is stored up for the righteous." — Proverbs 13:22 (NASB)

When people look at my life today, they see the success, the stages, the stars, and the spotlight. They see the bodyguard to celebrities, the executive, the film producer, the man who walks into rooms where few are allowed. What they do not see are the years it took to get here. The heartbreak I endured. The faith it took to survive. The children I raised. The integrity I protected. And the character I refused to compromise, no matter how much the world tried to break it.

My career in the entertainment industry began with muscle, but it grew through mastery. As a bodyguard, I was more than a shield. I was a presence. A strategist. A counselor. And in many ways, a silent protector in rooms where both fame and danger lived side by side. I have protected high-profile artists, political figures, and global icons, but what I learned went beyond security. I learned how to read people. I learned how to move through chaos with control. I learned that the biggest threats do not always come with fists. Sometimes they come with contracts, whispers, and fake smiles.

Later, I stepped into the role of a manager and executive. I found joy in building others up. I helped artists find their sound, their stage, and their voice. I stood behind platinum records and national tours, but I always kept my feet grounded. I never chased clout. I chased legacy. I made sure that everything I touched had purpose. That everything I built stood on truth.

But nothing has grounded me more than being a father and a grandfather. I look at my daughter, and I see the future. I see everything I wanted to be when I was young. I see my values, my spirit, and my love for God reflected back in her eyes. She has made me proud beyond words. My son-in-law stands like a man of strength and loyalty. And my grandsons give me hope that our family line will rise with pride, not pain.

I could not have raised my daughter the way I did without the help of my parents. They were very instrumental in her life, and I honor them for that. Their involvement gave me the space and the freedom to build everything I was building. While I was making critical moves in the entertainment industry and laying the groundwork for our future, they made sure my daughter always had love, support, and stability. It was a family effort, and I am forever grateful.

I take pride in breaking the curse that many men in our communities carry. I showed up. I stayed present. I kept my word. I did not allow my circumstances to become excuses. I made a conscious decision to lead with consistency, with compassion, and with the kind of love that builds strength instead of fear. I gave my daughter what every child deserves — a father who chooses them daily, even when life gets hard.

And above all, I chose God.

My spiritual foundation has been the one thing no one could ever take from me. I have been lied on, betrayed, disrespected, and targeted. But I have never been abandoned by the One who created me. God has been my anchor. He has guided me through the fire and taught me how to walk without getting burned.

There were nights I cried alone. There were days I questioned the journey. But every time I prayed, I felt a peace that silenced the noise. I knew I was chosen for something greater. I knew my story was not over. And I knew that Monte's attempts to tear me down were only sharpening my testimony.

Now, when I walk into boardrooms, when I stand behind a stage, or when I teach in my academy, I do it with power and purpose. Because I am not here just to be seen. I am here to plant seeds that will grow long after I am gone.

To the reader who has been balancing success and suffering, know this. You can win in both the spotlight and in silence. You can build your career and still build your family. You can succeed without selling your soul. And most of all, you can walk with God in every room you enter.

I have lived many lives, protector, executive, teacher, father, believer. But through them all, I have kept one promise to myself. I will never let what hurt me stop me from helping someone else.

That is the legacy I am building. One chapter at a time.

# Chapter 27

## Breaking Barriers

"The Lord was with Joseph and extended kindness to him, and gave him favor in the sight of the chief jailer." — Genesis 39:21 (NASB)

Most people would not believe it if they heard it. A Black man, standing in rooms surrounded by old-world Italians. Not as a guest. Not as hired help. But as a trusted protector. As one of them. I was a bodyguard for The Mob — not in theory or rumor, but in reality. And that experience changed the way I saw the world.

The Mob is a world rooted in loyalty, code, tradition, and silence. Outsiders do not get close. Especially not Black men. For decades, the Italian underworld was built on exclusion. You could work around them, but never inside. That rule did not apply to me. Why? Because I earned their respect the way respect is supposed to be earned. Not through fear, but through honor. Not by loud talk, but by quiet consistency. I showed up when I said I would. I handled myself like a professional. And most of all, I kept my mouth shut and my eyes open.

In a world where everything was about trust, I became the man they trusted to stand watch. I was at events, meetings, and private functions where only family was allowed. And still, they called me brother. Not out of charity, but out of recognition. That is rare. That is sacred.

Some of them told me straight to my face, "We don't deal with many Black men. But you, you're different." They said it without shame, because in their world, race was a barrier that only certain men could break. I was one of them. I never forgot the weight of that statement. I knew what it meant. I knew I had crossed an invisible line that most people never even get close to.

What they saw in me was what I had worked my whole life to become. A man of presence. A man of strength. A man of discipline. I did not need to speak for people to listen. I carried myself with a standard that said, "You can trust me." That was my protection. That was my weapon.
And that is what gave me access.

I witnessed things most people only see in movies. Deals made without a single word. Loyalty tested in subtle ways. Codes honored without a second thought. It taught me something deeper about human nature. Respect is the real currency. Not money. Not fame. Not power. Respect.

I never had to compromise who I was to be accepted in their circle. In fact, I stood out more because I stayed true to myself. I brought my own culture, my own history, and my own story into a world that had never made space for it. And they respected me more for it.

That experience shaped how I moved in every industry afterward. In business. In entertainment. In security. I learned how to walk into a room and read the temperature. I learned how to listen before I speak. I learned how to survive in spaces that were not designed for me.

And in many ways, I learned what it truly meant to break a barrier. Not by demanding inclusion. But by showing up with excellence until they could no longer deny me.

To the reader who has ever felt excluded, unseen, or unwanted — understand this. You do not need to be loud to be powerful. You do not need permission to be great. And you do not need acceptance to walk in purpose. Sometimes, your very presence will challenge the room.

Let it.

Because when you carry yourself with excellence, when you speak with clarity, when you move with confidence and honor, even the hardest walls will eventually make room for you.

I broke through one of the oldest cultural barriers in American history. And I did it not by becoming less of who I am, but by standing firmly in all that God made me to be.

That is the power of presence. That is the proof of purpose.

# Chapter 28

## When Celebration Revealed Character

"Let love be without hypocrisy. Abhor what is evil; cling to what is good." — Romans 12:9 (NASB)

It was supposed to be a weekend of celebration. A time to feel loved, honored, and appreciated. And it was, for the most part. The Mob threw me a birthday celebration I will never forget. It was first-class in every way. They didn't just acknowledge me. They honored me. They gave me my flowers while I was still breathing, and they did it with style, class, and generosity.

The Hilton casino rolled out the red carpet. Every guest I invited — family, friends, colleagues — was given a luxury hotel suite, completely free of charge, for three nights. That kind of gesture is rare. It spoke to how much respect I had earned, not just through words but through years of loyalty, integrity, and service. Joe Sarnese and Mike made sure everything was handled. I didn't have to lift a finger. It was their way of saying, "We see you. We value you."

The birthday dinner was held at Michael's restaurant, a fine dining spot known for its elegance and exclusivity. Around thirty people filled the private dining room. The air was filled with warmth and laughter. We shared stories, toasted to life, and broke bread like family. There was cake, ice cream, and conversation. And in that moment, I wanted everyone present to feel included.

Monte and my niece were both there. It happened to be their birthdays too. Out of love and humility, I had their names added to the cake. That was my heart. No matter the past, I still chose kindness. I even gave each of them a personal token of love to honor their day. I wanted unity. I wanted healing. I wanted to celebrate all of us.

And for that one night, it seemed like everything was peaceful. But peace is often short-lived when jealousy is present.
The very next day, Monte's true nature surfaced again. Mutual friends called me and told me everything he said behind my back. He trashed the restaurant, calling the food terrible and the service unprofessional. He belittled the atmosphere, the experience, and worst of all, he ridiculed me — the very person who made sure he was included, respected, and celebrated.

What bothered me most was not the critique. It was the spirit behind it. He was not offering feedback. He was poisoning the well. While others were still savoring the memory, Monte was trying to stain it with bitterness. His jealousy could not be contained. And everyone saw it.

Several friends who were present reached out and said the same thing: "Do not invite Monte to anything else. His mentality is toxic. That man is not capable of genuine joy for anyone but himself."

That moment confirmed what I had known for a long time. No matter how many times I extend grace, Monte will always choose to bite the hand that lifts him. Some people cannot handle someone else being honored, especially when they live in the shadow of comparison. Monte's reaction was not about the food. It was not about the hotel. It was not even about the celebration. It was about me being celebrated in a way he never had been.

But I do not throw celebrations to make anyone feel small. I do it to honor what God has done in my life. I do it to share the moment with the people I love. I do it to show that with faith, discipline, and favor, anything is possible.

To the reader, let this be a lesson. Sometimes the very people you include are the ones secretly resenting you the most. Not because you hurt them, but because your light exposes their emptiness.

I walked away from that birthday with more than memories. I walked away with confirmation. Confirmation that I am blessed. Confirmation that I am surrounded by people who see my worth. And confirmation that some relationships were never meant to sit at the table, no matter how many times you pull out a chair.

The celebration was beautiful. The betrayal was predictable. But neither will define me. My character will.

# Chapter 29

## The Release

"Cast all your anxiety on Him, because He cares for you." — 1 Peter 5:7 (NASB)

There comes a time in every journey when you stop asking why. You stop hoping for apologies that will never come. You stop replaying the betrayal and trying to understand it. You stop waiting for the person who broke you to finally see the damage they caused. Instead, you breathe. You reflect. And then, you release.

For most of my life, I carried Monte. Not just as a twin. Not just as a brother. But as a burden. I carried his insecurities. I carried the weight of his jealousy. I carried the pain of his attacks, both public and private. I defended him even when he did not deserve it. I tried to include him even when he tried to destroy me. I showed him grace, again and again, thinking that maybe one day he would get it. That maybe love would reach him. That maybe truth would heal him.

But some people do not want to be healed. They want to remain broken, so they have an excuse to keep breaking others. That realization changed everything for me.

I used to ask myself, "How can someone who came into the world with me hate me so deeply?" I looked for the root. Was it competition? Was it childhood wounds? Was it favoritism? But I have learned that sometimes evil is not about logic. Sometimes, it is about spirit. And you cannot fix what you did not break.

So I stopped trying to fix Monte. I stopped defending myself. I stopped giving him energy. And I started doing something I had never done before.

I released him.

I released him from my expectations. I released him from my prayers for his approval. I released the need to be understood by someone who never tried to understand me. I released the guilt of walking away. I released the grief of having a brother in body, but never in bond.

This was not about revenge. This was not about bitterness. This was about survival.

I realized I was pouring clean water into a leaking vessel. No matter how much love I gave him, it would never fill the emptiness in his soul. That is between him and God. I am not his fixer. I am not his keeper. I am a man who fought for peace and finally found it by walking away.

The moment I released Monte, something shifted inside me. My spirit felt lighter. My mind felt clearer. I no longer woke up wondering what falsehood he would spread next. I no longer checked my surroundings for his sabotage. I simply let go. Not because he deserved peace. But because I did.

You cannot build your future with hands tied to your past. You cannot fly when you are carrying someone else's poison. Letting go does not mean you are weak. It means you are wise.

To the reader holding on to someone who refuses to grow, learn this from me. You can love someone and still walk away. You can forgive someone and still guard your heart. You can honor the history without surrendering your destiny.

I am no longer fighting Monte. I am fighting for me. For my peace. For my joy. For my purpose. For the legacy I am building for my family. And I refuse to allow one broken man to steal another second of my light.

Let this be the chapter where I say goodbye to what was. And hello to what is waiting for me. I am free. I am focused. And I am finally done carrying what God never told me to carry.
That is the release.

# Chapter 30

## From Broken to Built

"And after you have suffered for a little while, the God of all grace, who called you to His eternal glory in Christ, will Himself perfect, confirm, strengthen, and establish you." — 1 Peter 5:10 (NASB)

The beautiful thing about being broken is that you get to rebuild. Piece by piece. Thought by thought. Step by step. You learn how to construct something stronger, wiser, and more purposeful than anything you had before.

I have lived through betrayal that would have buried most men. I have been attacked by the one person who should have protected me. I have had to rebuild my name, my reputation, and my spirit — not once, but over and over again. But each time, I came back with more power than I lost.

Because I was never just surviving. I was becoming.

When I finally released Monte and everything attached to him, a new space opened inside me. It was not just space for peace. It was space for purpose. I realized that everything I endured was not wasted. It was preparation.

Today, I walk as a man who is no longer just recovering. I am leading. I am mentoring. I am building systems, businesses, and programs that help others navigate pain the way I had to — with truth, integrity, and God.

I created The Shaolin Experience Academy not just as a martial arts school, but as a sanctuary for the broken, the overlooked, and the discouraged. I built Burno-Patterson Entertainment Group to give artists, athletes, and entrepreneurs real leadership and honest representation. I co-founded companies not to flex, but to create safe spaces for growth, restoration, and excellence. Every contract I sign, every deal I make, every young person I mentor is a living answer to the pain I endured.

I am not ashamed of my past. It gave me wisdom. I am not bitter about my scars. They gave me vision. And I am not hiding from my truth. It gave me purpose.

What once nearly destroyed me is now the fuel behind my movement. I do not just want to heal myself. I want to help others break the silence, overcome the shame, and build lives of legacy and freedom.

That is why this book is not just a memoir. It is a blueprint. It is a call to every person who has ever been lied on, overlooked, abused, or broken by someone they trusted. I am here to tell you that healing is possible. Strength is possible. Legacy is possible.

But it does not happen by accident. It happens by choice.

You must choose to rise. You must choose to walk away from what keeps you broken. You must choose to invest in your future instead of remaining trapped in your past.

I chose to build.

I chose to let my pain become my platform, my testimony become my tool, and my name become something my daughter and grandsons can be proud of.

The world may have watched me suffer, but now they will witness me soar.

And when my documents, certificates, letters from leaders like President Obama, and everything I have accomplished are seen in these pages, let them serve as proof. Not of arrogance, but of overcoming. Not of titles, but of truth. Not of status, but of perseverance.

Because what was once broken has now been built. And I am just getting started.

# Chapter 31

## I Love You My Brother

"But I say to you, love your enemies and pray for those who persecute you." — Matthew 5:44 (NASB)

I never imagined it would come to this. Not with you. Not with someone who came into the world with me. We shared a womb, a name, a history. We were twins. People used to say we were inseparable. But they never saw the cracks beneath the surface. They never heard the words you whispered behind my back. They never knew that my greatest heartbreak would not come from an enemy, but from my own brother.

You did not just betray me. You tried to erase me. You lied on me to churches, to courts, to people I loved. You weaponized your pain and aimed it at my peace. You painted me as a villain so you could wear the mask of the victim. You spoke death over my name while I was praying for your healing. You hurt me in ways that words cannot capture.

And yet, I love you.

I do not say that lightly. I say it with tears in my eyes and truth in my chest. I love you because God requires it of me. I love you because I refuse to let your hate turn my heart cold. I love you because I understand something now. You are sick. And the sickness is not just emotional. It is spiritual. It is generational. It is a wound that you never gave God a chance to heal.

I watched you destroy relationships, sabotage love, disrespect our parents, and insult the very people who helped you. You took and took until there was nothing left to give. And when I stood up to protect myself, you called me the enemy.

But even then, I kept praying for you.

You have said horrible things about me. You tried to turn others against me. You called the police, filed false claims, and stood in court with lies dripping from your tongue. And I still asked God to cover you.

Because I know the truth.

You do not hate me because of anything I did. You hate me because I survived. You hate me because I became everything you could not. You hate me because I remind you of the man you should have been.

But here is what I want you to know.
I release you. Fully. Completely. You no longer have power over my thoughts, my peace, or my path. I will not carry your rage into my future. I will not carry your lies into my legacy. I choose to walk in light while you hide in shadows.

And even now, I choose love.

You may never apologize. You may never heal. But I will not allow your brokenness to break me.

I leave you with words from a song that inspired me, written by Raymond Reeder. It captured what I felt when my own words fell short.

You tried to bury me, but I am the seed. I grew stronger. I grew wiser. I built a life rooted in truth, love, and God. I wrote this book not to shame you, but to finally free myself.

And this final chapter, this final message, is not a curse. It is a covering. I love you my brother. I always did.

But now, I love you from a distance.

I pray you get the help you need. I pray one day you wake up and realize how much love you were given. And I pray that when your pride fades, you will look back and remember the brother who gave you chance after chance.

But until then, I walk away with peace. I walk away with purpose. And I walk away with my heart still open.

Because love always wins. And this is my final act of love.

# Chapter 32

## I'm Still Here

Scripture: Job 1:8

"And the Lord said unto Satan, Hast thou considered my servant Job, that there is none like him in the earth, a perfect and an upright man, one that feareth God, and escheweth evil?"

There were days I wanted to give up.

Not because I was weak, but because I was tired.

Tired of being lied on, set up, betrayed, misunderstood, attacked, and judged by people who never once asked for my side.

Tired of being the strong one, the dependable one, the one who always held it together. Tired of forgiving while silently bleeding inside.

I took every hit.

I buried my pain to protect others.

I stayed silent while enemies slandered my name, weaponized my kindness, and mocked the heart that only tried to save them.

But despite it all, I'm still here. Yes, my scars are internal.
They do not show up in photographs.

They are stitched into memory, wrapped in silence, and carried with grace. But I wear them like a crown now, not a curse.
Everything the enemy meant for evil, God flipped for my good. They tried to bury me. They did not know I was a seed.

They tried to destroy my reputation, not knowing my favor was not man-made. They tried to cancel me, but purpose cannot be canceled. I am a living, breathing testimony that what God ordains, no lie can stop. I faced betrayals that would've broken most men.
But they did not break me — they built me. Every courtroom battle. Every sleepless night. Every false accusation. Every smear campaign. Every slammed door.
Each one taught me how to stand, how to fight, and most of all, how to heal. Some people only loved me when I was broken.
They applauded my pain because it made them feel powerful.

But the moment I stood tall, restored, whole, and walking in divine alignment, the attacks intensified.

But hear me clearly — the devil had to get permission.

You cannot touch what belongs to God without divine clearance.

So if you're reading this while going through your own silent storm, remember this: The size of your battle is a preview of the blessing on the other side.
If the enemy is trying hard to stop you, it's because what you carry is unstoppable. I'm not bitter.
I'm not broken. I'm not hiding. I'm still here.
I survived what was meant to silence me. I overcame what was meant to end me.
And I am walking forward not with revenge, but with peace, power, and purpose. And as Methrone sings so perfectly in the song that follows this story:
"I'm still here."

It is more than a lyric. It is a declaration.
It is a triumph.

It is a reminder to every enemy, every doubter, every hater, and even to myself — I made it. And I am just getting started.

They asked, how did he survive that? They wondered, how is he still standing?

If you've read this far, you know the answer — because God had His hand on me the entire time.

Monte tried everything.

He tried to assassinate my character, steal my identity, and strip me of every blessing I built. He used lies, courtrooms, fake pastors, slanderous emails, and even law enforcement.
He played victim while swinging the sword.

He brought darkness into places meant to be sacred — family gatherings, holidays, and even funerals.

But I'm still here.

I survived betrayal by my own blood.

I endured accusations that could've ended my career.

I stood in courtrooms where lies echoed louder than truth. I kept my mouth shut when my spirit screamed to speak.
I stayed loyal to a family system that didn't always return the loyalty.

Still I rose — because God saw something in me, just like He saw in Job. I know what it's like to be targeted for simply being chosen.
I know what it's like to be called everything but your name.

To be misunderstood by those who should've known you best. To

walk into rooms heavy with whispers and jealousy.
But none of it broke me. It made me stronger.
It made me wiser.
It made me dangerous to the enemy — because now, I don't just survive, I thrive. Like Job, I lost a lot.
I lost trust.
I lost time.

I lost relationships I thought were solid. But also like Job, I gained more than I lost. I gained clarity.
I gained favor.

I gained a legacy that cannot be taken, tarnished, or told by anyone but me. Now the same people who tried to bury me have to watch me bloom.
This chapter is not just for me.

It's for every person who was counted out. For those betrayed by someone close.
For anyone who almost gave up when the pain felt heavier than the purpose.

Let this be your proof — you can survive anything when God is in the fight with you. When Satan went before God, he didn't ask to destroy the weak.
He asked to test the strongest.

God didn't recommend Job because he was fragile.

He recommended him because He knew he wouldn't fold. I know now that God said the same about me.
Hast thou considered my servant Lamar? I don't take that lightly.
I don't wear my survival as arrogance.

I wear it as proof of what happens when you trust God through the storm. You might lose some things.
You might cry some nights.

You might feel invisible or misunderstood.

But if you stay grounded in purpose, your victory will outshine their lies. So here I am.
At the end of this book, but the beginning of a movement. Still alive. Still sane. Still rising. Still favored. Still here.

# About the Author

Lamar Burno Sr. is a father, grandfather, Executive Protection Specialist, and seasoned entrepreneur whose life has spanned military service, law enforcement, entertainment, and the martial arts. With over three decades of firsthand experience protecting high-profile clients, producing film and music projects, and building successful companies, Lamar brings unmatched discipline, resilience, and insight to every endeavor he undertakes.

He is the founder and CEO of Burno-Patterson Entertainment Group, Burno-Patterson Sports Management, Casa Lucas Spirits, and On Point Executive Protection. His work has brought him alongside Grammy- and Emmy-winning artists, as well as major names in film and television. As an actor and stunt coordinator, Lamar has appeared in NY Undercover and co-starred with Denzel Washington in the film Fallen.

A highly respected martial artist, Lamar holds black belts and master-level ranks in Hung Gar Kung Fu, Tae Kwon Do, and Ninjitsu. He founded The Shaolin Experience, a school dedicated to preserving traditional martial arts while empowering the next generation through discipline and self-mastery.

A proud native of Elizabethtown, North Carolina, Lamar is also deeply rooted in community service. He has served in the U.S. Army as a Military Police Officer, worked with the Philadelphia School District Police, and held leadership roles in organizations like the Masonic Order and the Guardian Angels.

In Shattered Bonds: A Brother's Betrayal, Lamar shares a raw, unfiltered account of betrayal, mental health struggles, and redemption. His powerful story is more than a memoir—it's a movement. One that sheds light on injustice, mental illness, and the strength it takes to overcome.

Lamar continues to speak across the country, uplifting audiences with a message of truth, faith, and healing. He remains a passionate advocate for mental health awareness, legal reform, and family reconciliation.

# U.S. PROTECTION SPECIALIST
## *AUTHORIZED PROTECTION AGENT*

This is the property of On Point Executive Protection. This Agent works under the direct laws of the U.S. Supreme Court and has the authority to protect and defend the U.S. Constitution. The Agent also has the right to transport prisoners, investigate crimes and bodyguard dignitaries thereof. This is not limited to only the United States, but internationally as well.

NAME: LAMONT B. BURNO
BADGE#: 7979

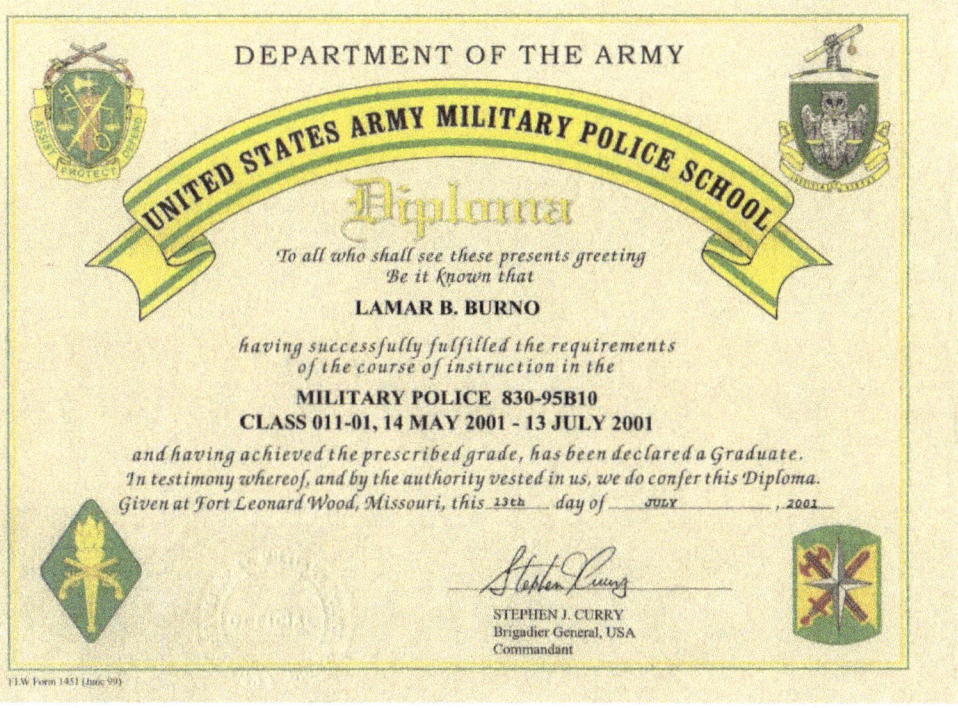

DEPARTMENT OF THE ARMY

UNITED STATES ARMY MILITARY POLICE SCHOOL

## Diploma

To all who shall see these presents greeting
Be it known that

**LAMAR B. BURNO**

having successfully fulfilled the requirements
of the course of instruction in the

**MILITARY POLICE 830-95B10**
**CLASS 011-01, 14 MAY 2001 - 13 JULY 2001**

and having achieved the prescribed grade, has been declared a Graduate.
In testimony whereof, and by the authority vested in us, we do confer this Diploma.
Given at Fort Leonard Wood, Missouri, this 13th day of ___JULY___ , 2001

STEPHEN J. CURRY
Brigadier General, USA
Commandant

FLW Form 1451 (June 99)

109

ARMY/ACE REGISTRY TRANSCRIPT SYSTEM

ISSUED: 5/3/2007          *** PERSONAL WEB TRANSCRIPT ***

Name: BURNO LAMAR BERNARD
Rank: PRIVATE FIRST CLASS, E3
Status: Inactive

AARTS ID: 2007-WB004306

| Military Course Completions |
|---|

Course: BASIC TRAINING                            ACE EXHIBIT: AR-2201-0399

(RECRUIT TRAINING)

Description: UPON COMPLETION OF THE COURSE, THE RECRUIT WILL BE ABLE TO DEMONSTRATE GENERAL KNOWLEDGE OF MILITARY ORGANIZATION AND CULTURE, MASTERY OF INDIVIDUAL AND GROUP COMBAT SKILLS INCLUDING MARKSMANSHIP AND FIRST AID, ACHIEVEMENT OF MINIMAL PHYSICAL CONDITIONING STANDARDS, AND APPLICATION OF BASIC SAFETY AND LIVING SKILLS IN AN OUTDOOR ENVIRONMENT. INSTRUCTION INCLUDES LECTURES, DEMONSTRATIONS, AND PERFORMANCE EXERCISES IN BASIC MILITARY CULTURE/SUBJECTS INCLUDING MARKSMANSHIP, PHYSICAL CONDITIONING, FIRST AID AND OUTDOOR ADAPTATION/LIVING SKILLS.

Recommendation: IN THE LOWER DIVISION BACCALAUREATE/ASSOCIATE DEGREE CATEGORY, 1 SEMESTER HOUR IN PERSONAL PHYSICAL CONDITIONING, 1 IN OUTDOOR SKILLS PRACTICUM, 1 IN MARKSMANSHIP, AND 1 IN FIRST AID.

Course Title: Light Weapons Infantryman Light Weapons Infantryman Phase 1, Phase 2, Prior Service          ACE Exhibit: AR-2201-0310

Location: US ARMY TRAINING CENTER at FT BENNING, GA          Army Course Number: 11B10-OSUT

From: 10/21/1991          To: 01/31/1992

Description: TO PREPARE PERSONNEL FOR INFANTRY UNITS. LECTURES, DEMONSTRATIONS, AND PRACTICAL EXERCISES COVER DISCIPLINE, MOTIVATION, AND PHYSICAL FITNESS. THIS COURSE IS OFFERED IN A 12-13 WEEK LONG PRESENTATION OR IN SPLIT TRAINING WHERE COURSE IS CONDUCTED AS TWO 6-7 WEEK LONG PHASES. THIS COURSE INCLUDES AN 8-9 WEEK LONG BASIC TRAINING COMPONENT.

Recommendations: CREDIT IS NOT RECOMMENDED BECAUSE OF THE MILITARY-SPECIFIC NATURE OF THE COURSE.

Course Title: Basic Military Internment/Resettlement Specialist Reclassification Military Police Reclassification          ACE Exhibit: AR-1728-0124

Location: US ARMY TRAINING CENTER at FT LEONARD WOOD, MO          Army Course Number: 830-95B10

From: 05/14/2001          To: 07/13/2001

Description: UPON COMPLETION OF THE COURSE, THE STUDENT WILL PERFORM PRISONER ADMINISTRATION AND SERVICES; EXERCISE SECURITY AND CONTROL; MOVE PRISONERS; DISCUSS CONTEMPORARY ISSUES IN CONFINEMENT FACILITIES, AND APPLY KNOWLEDGE OF LAW

ENFORCEMENT OPERATIONS TO PATROL PROCEDURES, TRAFFIC ENFORCEMENT, FIRST RESPONDER INVESTIGATIONS, AND SPECIAL OPERATIONS TO CONFORM TO CONSTITUTIONAL STANDARDS. LECTURES AND PRACTICAL EXERCISES COVER INTRODUCTORY METHODS OF LAW ENFORCEMENT OPERATIONS AND USE A MOCK CONFINEMENT FACILITY TO INTRODUCE CORRECTIONS SUBJECTS AND PROCEDURES.

Recommendations: IN THE LOWER-DIVISION BACCALAUREATE/ASSOCIATE DEGREE CATEGORY, 3 SEMESTER HOURS IN INTRODUCTION TO CORRECTIONS OR 3 IN LAW ENFORCEMENT.

| Test Scores |
|---|
| ——————————————— NONE ——————————————— |
| Military Experience |

| Military Occupational Specialties Held: | 11B10 | Primary | From: 03/1992 | To: 07/2001 |
|---|---|---|---|---|
| | 11B10 | Duty | | |
| | 11B40 | Duty | | |
| | 11B10 | Secondary | | |

Military Occupational Specialty Group 11B                                    ACE Guide Number

Title: INFANTRYMAN                                                                         MOS 11B-004

SQT (Thru Oct 1991)/SDT (Nov 1991 thru Feb 1995) Taken: None

Description of 11B10: USES INDIVIDUAL INFANTRY WEAPONS; LAYS FIELD WIRE; PERFORMS BASIC COMMUNICATIONS FUNCTIONS AND OPERATES COMMUNICATION EQUIPMENT; UTILIZES CAMOUFLAGE TO CONCEAL WEAPONS AND PERSONNEL; CONSTRUCTS MINOR FORTIFICATIONS; PERFORMS LAND NAVIGATION; PERFORMS PREVENTIVE MAINTENANCE ON WEAPONS, EQUIPMENT, AND SOME VEHICLES; MAKES VERBAL REPORTS; ADMINISTERS FIRST AID; OPERATES WHEELED VEHICLES TO TRANSPORT PERSONNEL, SUPPLIES, AND EQUIPMENT.

ACE Credit Recommendation for 11B10: IN THE VOCATIONAL CERTIFICATE CATEGORY, 3 SEMESTER HOURS IN MECHANICAL MAINTENANCE. IN THE LOWER-DIVISION BACCALAUREATE/ASSOCIATE DEGREE CATEGORY, 1 SEMESTER HOUR IN MAP READING, 1 IN FIRST AID, AND CREDIT IN SURVEYING ON THE BASIS OF INSTITUTIONAL EVALUATION (10/83).

Military Occupational Specialty Group 11B                                    ACE Guide Number

Title: Infantryman                                                                          MOS 11B-005

SQT (Thru Oct 1991)/SDT (Nov 1991 thru Feb 1995) Taken: None

Description of 11B40: USES INDIVIDUAL INFANTRY WEAPONS; LAYS FIELD WIRE; PERFORMS BASIC COMMUNICATIONS FUNCTIONS AND OPERATES COMMUNICATION EQUIPMENT; UTILIZES CAMOUFLAGE TO CONCEAL WEAPONS AND PERSONNEL; CONSTRUCTS MINOR FORTIFICATIONS; PERFORMS LAND NAVIGATION; PERFORMS PREVENTIVE MAINTENANCE ON WEAPONS, EQUIPMENT, AND SOME VEHICLES; MAKES VERBAL REPORTS; ADMINISTERS FIRST AID; OPERATES WHEELED VEHICLES TO TRANSPORT PERSONNEL, SUPPLIES, AND EQUIPMENT. SERVES AS A TEAM LEADER, DIRECTING DEPLOYMENT AND EMPLOYMENT OF PERSONNEL; SUPERVISES MAINTENANCE AND CONSTRUCTION ACTIVITIES; READS, INTERPRETS, AND COLLECTS INTELLIGENCE INFORMATION; DISTRIBUTES ADMINISTRATIVE AND TRAINING DOCUMENTS; TRAINS SUBORDINATE PERSONNEL. AS A FIRST-LINE SUPERVISOR, DIRECTS THE UTILIZATION OF PERSONNEL AND EQUIPMENT; COORDINATES UNIT ACTIONS WITH ADJACENT AND SUPPORTING ELEMENTS; INSURES PROPER COLLECTION AND REPORTING OF INTELLIGENCE DATA. SUPERVISES AND TRAINS PERSONNEL IN INFANTRY OPERATIONS AND INTELLIGENCE ACTIVITIES; ASSISTS IN PLANNING, ORGANIZING, DIRECTING, SUPERVISING, TRAINING, COORDINATING, AND REPORTING ACTIVITIES OF SUBORDINATE UNITS; SUPERVISES RECEIPT, STORAGE, AND DISTRIBUTION OF SUPPLIES, EQUIPMENT, AND FOOD TO SUBORDINATE UNITS; PROVIDES ORAL AND WRITTEN REPORTS; ASSISTS IN PRODUCTION AND ADMINISTRATION OF STAFF JOURNALS, FILES, RECORDS, AND REPORTS.

ACE Credit Recommendation for 11B40: IN THE VOCATIONAL CERTIFICATE CATEGORY, 3 SEMESTER HOURS IN MECHANICAL MAINTENANCE. IN THE LOWER-DIVISION BACCALAUREATE/ASSOCIATE DEGREE CATEGORY, 2 SEMESTER HOURS IN MAP READING, 1 IN FIRST AID, 3 IN RECORD KEEPING, 3 IN PERSONNEL SUPERVISION, 3 IN HUMAN RELATIONS, 3 IN PRINCIPLES OF INSTRUCTION, AND CREDIT IN SURVEYING ON THE BASIS OF INSTITUTIONAL EVALUATION. IN THE UPPER-DIVISION

Treasures of the Heart International Ministries
dba Crystal Rain Institute
115 Folly Ct., Fayetteville, NC 28356-1006
(910) 286-9436


January 15, 2021


Dear Honorable Judge,

Please accept this letter as a testament to the character of one Mr. Lamont Bershawn Burno.
Your honor I received an inbox from Lamont in June of 2010 on a social Media platform named
"TAGGED." He began talking about a ministry he wanted to get off the ground. He also said he
was looking for a wife, and spoke of a reality show entitled "The Bishop's Wife."

Your Honor, I helped as much as I could from California. When I needed more information
about the ministry Lamont would become angry. I cautioned him to control his anger and vulgar
language. I began to look into his "Bishopric." As an Archbishop, I know the process it takes to
become a Bishop. To my surprise, I found that Lamont was not a real Bishop in the Lord's
Church, or the ministry "I Found My Rib" was only on social media, he was no songwriter for
celebrities, or concert promoter" in Wyncote, PA, or any state. When I confronted him about his
flagrant lies, he slandered me, my name and ministry; threatened me, and vowed to always
make my life a living hell. (In which he's done!).


In February of 2011, Lamont began to act very strange. He had started talking about his brother.
I knew about his oldest brother, but he said he had a twin. This was out of the blue. He was
angry, threatening and accusatory. Lamont said he wished his brother was dead and felt as if
Lamar wanted his life. I said " this is common amongst twins Lamont." I hadn't met Lamar, as
of today I've never met Lamont. I believe I had a conversation with Lamont on or about
February 21, 2011 in which I received disrespect, names calling, threats and more.


After being abused by him, and his girlfriend, I contacted the authorities. The Stanislaus County
Sheriff's Department spoke with Lamont Burno, and determined from that conversation that he
had in fact harassed me. I was given a report number; they also made contact with a Detective
Mata from the Cheltenham PD.

I eventually received a call from Mr. Lamar Bernard Burno in May of 2012. We had a conversation, and he assured me that they had Lamont under some control at that time. Well, Lamont broke away from that control and began to destroy every life around him, especially Lamar. He has drug his brother through the ringer for no reason at all. Lamar has become his target, and I fear for Lamar's life. I urge you to take heed before we witness an unnecessary death due to untreated mental illness. I believe there is a need for a court ordered psychological evaluation.

The last conversation I had with Lamont was in early 2013. My phone was ringing as if it was a ringback, but I never called his line. Anyway, we spoke, and I said "I finally spoke with your brother Lamar; immediately. Lamont hit the ceiling and said "If you're going to talk to that M***f**r, don't ever talk to me again, and if you f*ck him, don't catch AIDS." I found that to be just awful, and hateful. Not even an hour later, I get a knock on my door, and it's the Stanislaus County Sheriff asking me if I knew Lamont. "I said "yes, I just answered a weird call in which I didn't place, there was no outbound call made from my phone." The officer stated that Lamont just called us and said "you" called and harassed him. I said, "I hesitated in answering the phone because it was his number, but I thought it could've been an emergency regarding his mother, who'd been ill. Needless to say, they gave me a report number H-115069. The report number in question was given to me by Officer John Harrison to protect me against Lamont Bershawn Burno. Had they confirmed the report number, the officers would have found that it was an existing harassment report written and issued by Officer Harrison after he ascertained that Lamont had an obvious problem with authority and harassment did occur. The officers stated that now you both can stay away from each other. I said "I never bothered him, and they seemed to not even hear me. I was dumbfounded. So I can only imagine what he said; but that fact still remains, it was my report number, that I was issued, and the same report number he put on page 6 of his book, in which he degraded his whole family, without their knowledge.

Your Honor, we are all rooting for Lamont Bershawn Burno to seek help for his outburst of anger, vulgar language, threats and lies. There are many that moved away, dumped the friendships, and have called the police because of his inappropriate actions. When is enough, enough?

Lamont has lived at home with his mother all his life, outside of attempting to join the military, to only be discharged after being on suicide watch. On the other hand, Lamar lives on his own, raised his daughter, and is now a grandfather, and a successful businessman.

Again, thank you for considering my testimony, and the possibility of Lamont getting some

much needed court ordered therapy. Let's do something now to avoid an unnecessary loss of life amongst family.


Humbly submitted,

*Dr. Danette M Vercher 1/15/2021*

Dr. Danette M. Vercher




Cumberland County,
North Carolina
Sworn to (or affirmed) and subscribed before me this day by

*Dr. Danette M Vercher*
Name of Principal.

_____
Name of Principal.

_____
Name of Principal.

Date: 1/15/21

Official Signature of Notary

*Reginald Lewis*
Notary's printed or typed name,
Notary Public
My commission expires: 2/24/25

120

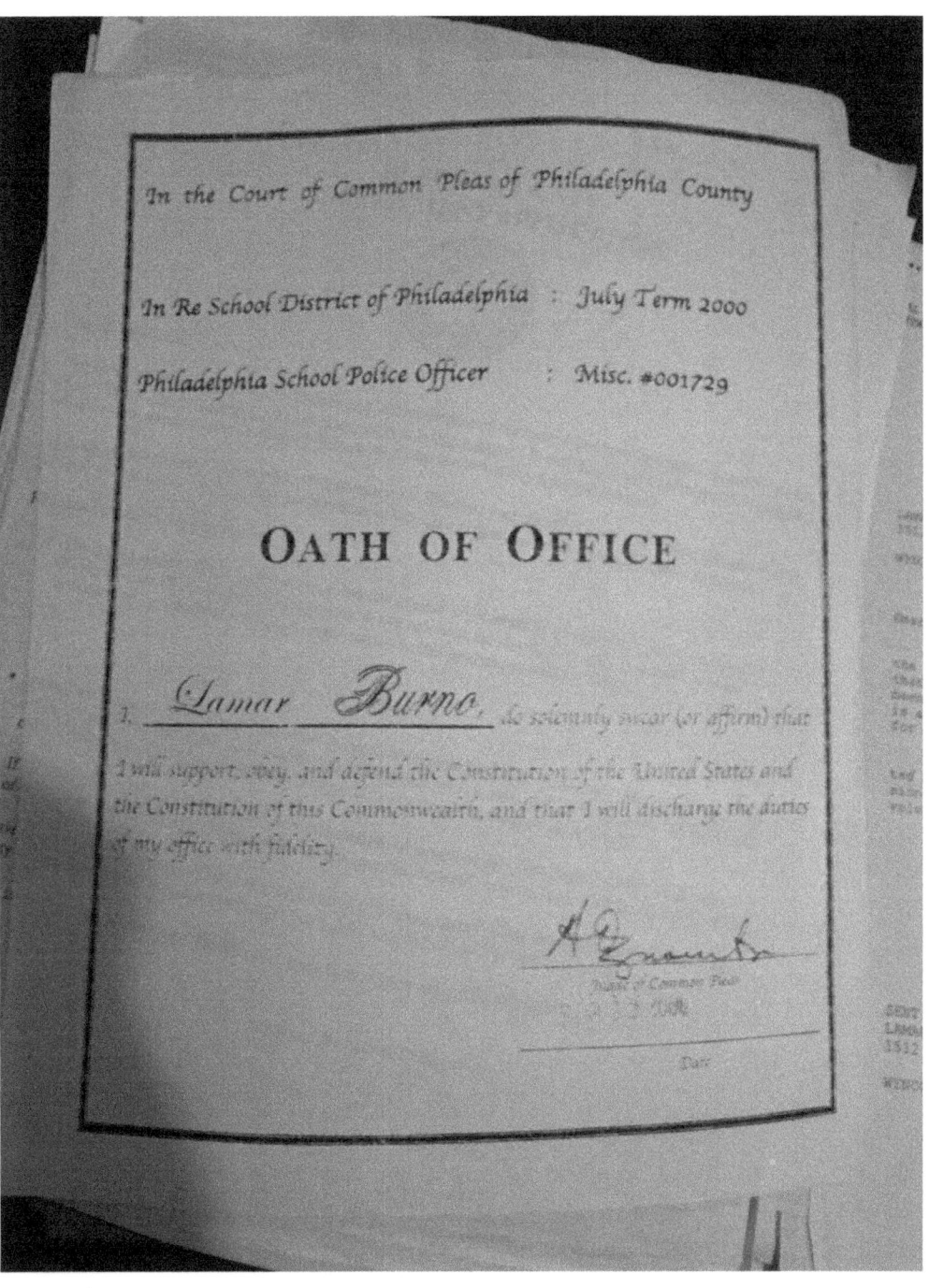

In the Court of Common Pleas of Philadelphia County

In Re School District of Philadelphia : July Term 2000

Philadelphia School Police Officer : Misc. #001729

# OATH OF OFFICE

I, _Lamar Burno_, do solemnly swear (or affirm) that I will support, obey, and defend the Constitution of the United States and the Constitution of this Commonwealth, and that I will discharge the duties of my office with fidelity.

_____
Judge of Common Pleas

_____
Date

Please review and respond as you deem appropriate.

From: Anonymous [mailto:anonymous@anonymous.us]
Sent: Saturday, December 01, 2012 4:47 PM
To: FDLE Comments
Subject: Comment from internet site user

WebSiteCommentsID: 2531

Your Email Address: minigrabstreet@yahoo.com

Your Name: Lamont Burno

Your Phone Number: 2672781875

Your Address / City / State / Zip: 1512 W. Church Rd.

Comments: To whom it may concern, It has been brought to my attention that a recent recruit of SEPSI named Lamar Bernard Burno has recently "Passed" the tests given & have received a certificate from Lake Technical Center for public safety completion. I've read all of the requirements that were necessary to enter into the program. I hereby acknowledge that Lamar B. Burno SSN: 243-31-9994 has NOT completed a full tour of military training & has NOT graduated from ANY college. Lamar has obtained the same FAKE degrees from "Youngsfield University" as Floridas current Chief of Police. I totally understand his hype into wanting to become a police officer/ state trooper, but I would also feel comfortable knowing (1) that Florida or any other law enforcement agency has fully investigated the backgrounds of their proposed employees (2) that the person carrying a gun/ firearm did so WITHOUT falsifying or fabricating documentation. Lamar has a terrible anger management problem, but would lie at all cost to be a law enforcement official. Lamar has also been convicted of (1) Simple Assault in Pa. (2) carrying a concealed weapon on casino property - NJ in which he was arrested & received probation. It is with my EVERY regard that this situation is NOT handled lightly. If this is NOT the correct authority to present this issue to please forward this email to the correct office. I think this is TOTALLY unfair to an individual who has better qualifications to be an officer of law.

Form inserted: 12/1/2012 4:47:28 PM

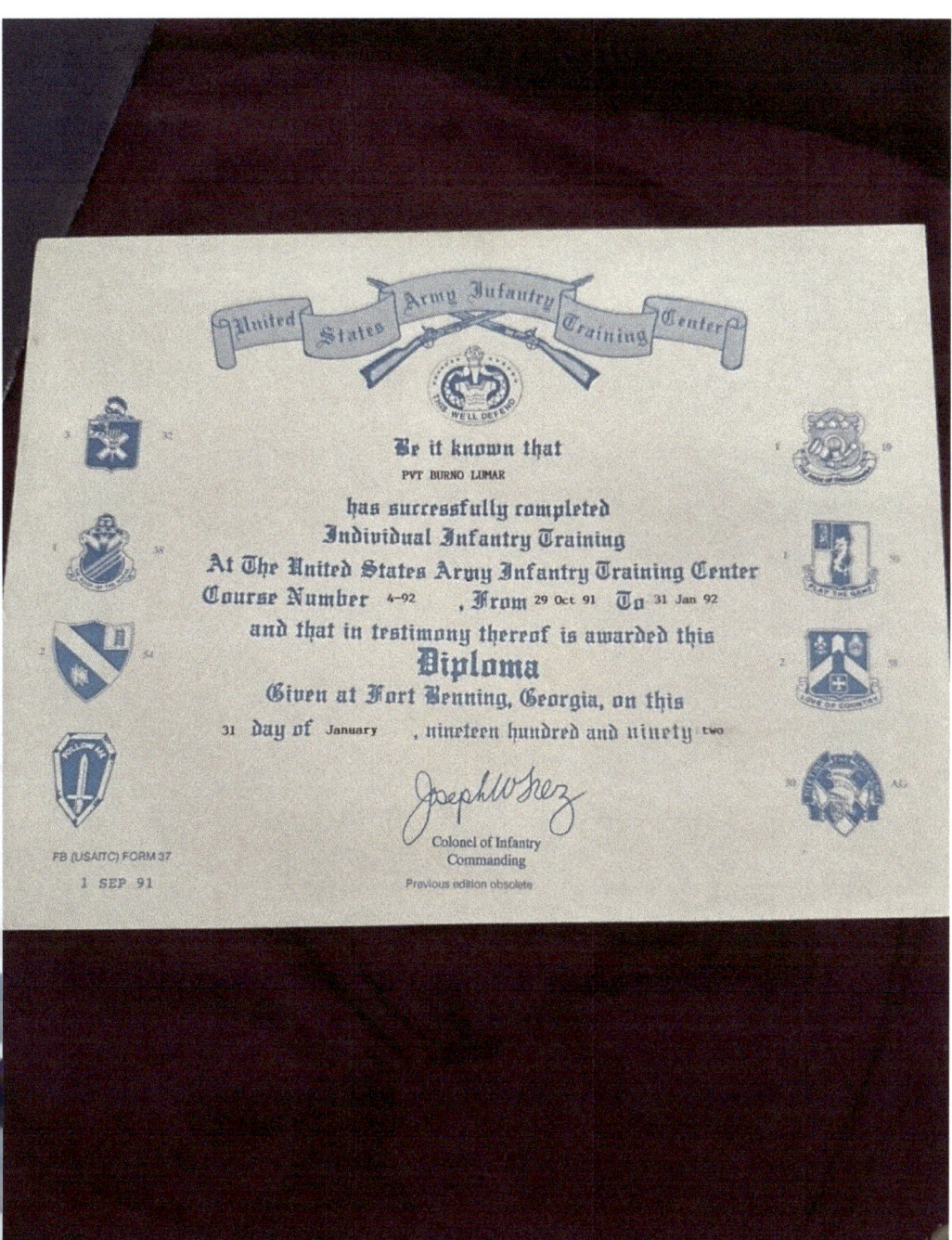

123

# Lake Technical Center

## Institute of Public Safety

This certifies that

## Lamar B. Burno

having satisfactorily completed all requirements as prescribed by the Department of Education for the State of Florida and the Lake Technical Center Charter Board of Lake County, Florida for

## Law Enforcement Officer Proficiency Course
### Class # 15-12-214-05

this 15th day of November, 2012, is therefore awarded this

### CERTIFICATE OF COMPLETION

_____
Criminal Justice Academy Director

_____
Lake Technical Center Director

anger, and I fear for Lamar's life. I urge you to take heed before we witness an unnecessary death due to untreated mental illness. I believe there is a need for a court ordered psychological evaluation.

The last conversation I had with Lamont was in early 2013. My phone was ringing as if it was a ringback, but I never called his line. Anyway, we spoke, and I said "I finally spoke with your brother Lamar, immediately. Lamont hit the ceiling and said "If you're going to talk to that M****f**r, don't ever talk to me again, and if you f*ck him, don't catch AIDS." I found that to be just awful, and hateful. Not even an hour later, I get a knock on my door, and it's the Stanislaus County Sheriff asking me if I knew Lamont. "I said "yes, I just answered a weird call in which I didn't place, there was no outbound call made from my phone." The officer stated that Lamont told them that I called and harassed him. I said, "I hesitated in answering the phone because it was his number, but I thought it could've been an emergency regarding his mother, who'd been ill. Needless to say, they gave me a report number, without confirming the report number I was given prior by Officer Richardson. Lamont lied and told them that he was given this number by the Sheriff's before. Had they confirmed it, it was the same report number Officer Richardson gave me for protection, after he ascertained that Lamont had an obvious problem with authority. The officers stated that now you both can stay away from each other. I said "I never bothered him, and they seemed to not even hear me. I was dumbfounded!

Your Honor, we are all rooting for Lamont Bershawn Burno to seek help for his outburst of anger, vulgar language, threats and lies. There are many that moved away, dumped the friendships, and have called the police because of his inappropriate actions. When is enough, enough?

Lamont has lived at home with his mother all his life, outside of attempting to join the military, to only be discharged after being on suicide watch. On the other hand, Lamar lives on his own, raised his daughter, and is now a grandfather, and a successful businessman.

Again, thank you for considering my testimony, and the possibility of Lamont getting some much needed court ordered therapy. Let's do something now to avoid an unnecessary loss of life amongst family.


Humbly submitted,


Dr. Danette M. Vercher

910-286-9436

**Description of Complaint:**

In the space below, tell us the nature of your complaint. Be sure to include all the facts that you want the Board to consider, including names, dates, and places. Use additional sheets if necessary. **Upload copies (not originals) of any documents that support your complaint.**

Mr. Fairley Newton Jr. is allowing Lamar Burno to embalm corpses and taking pictures with his cell phone in order to make people think/believe that he's a licensed embalmer. Lamar is a sociopath, convicted felon and suffers from HPD (Histrionic Personality Disorder). Lamar is very manipulative, charismatic and believable to those people that don't know him.

The underline reason that Lamar resides in Elizabethtown, NC is because he was ordered to have supervised probation from being convicted of "Uttered Forged Instrument" in Lake County Florida having probation transferred from Montgomery County, PA to Elizabethtown, NC.

Lamar has traveled with Fairley Newton Jr. several funeral homes assisting him in embalming bodies to the point that one evening Lamar stopped by my home in Fayetteville carrying the embalming fluid in the glass container. I told him to leave it outside and not to bring it inside this home.

I'm not sure if Lamar created a fake license and showed Fairley Newton Jr. and he just never took the time to do the research on the license number, but Lamar is a transporter for the funeral home as well as an embalmer or what Lamar considers an "Embalming Specialist."

Some of the funeral homes consist of Cunningham in Fayetteville, Majestic Funeral Home, Johnson Funeral Home and others.

I, the undersigned, hereby submit the above complaint, and attest that it is true and accurate to the best of my recollection. I agree to cooperate by furnishing to the representatives of the Board all pertinent or requested information and records in my possession concerning the alleged misconduct of the person or entity against whom I have complained. I further agree that I will testify as a witness if a hearing is held concerning the alleged misconduct of the person or entity against whom I have complained.

I understand that my identity will be disclosed to the funeral establishment/crematory/person against whom I have complained. I understand that anonymous complaints will not be processed. I understand that, except in limited circumstances, North Carolina public records laws require that copies of complaints and responses be made available to anyone who requests them.

I understand that the Board cannot give me legal advice, cannot represent me or intervene on my behalf in any court proceeding, and cannot provide any opinions or make any determinations regarding civil liability. I understand that if I believe I have suffered damages because of an act or omission of a licensee of the Board, I should not wait for the Board's disposition of a consumer complaint before pursuing any legal claim or seeking legal advice.

**Signature:**

*Lamont Bershuwn*

**Date:**                    04/22/2024

# Citation

WHEREAS, **Lamar Burno** has served our Nation honorably for seven years as a military police officer; and,

WHEREAS, **Lamar Burno** is a leader in his religious community, being ordained Reverend of the Pentecostal Faith since 1997; and,

WHEREAS, **Lamar Burno** is a member of the Philadelphia Chapter of the Guardian Angels, where he has trained Pennsylvania and New Jersey's members in self-defense; and,

WHEREAS, **Lamar Burno** has assisted the Atlantic City Police and community in criminal investigations as a Guardian Angel; and,

WHEREAS, **Lamar Burno** has protected Philadelphia students, staff, and facilities as a Philadelphia School Police Officer; and,

THEREFORE, in presenting this citation to:

## MR. LAMAR BURNO

I, **Frank R. Lautenberg**, United States Senator, on behalf of the People of the State of New Jersey hereby congratulate you on your contributions to your community and to the State of New Jersey.

FRANK R. LAUTENBERG

October 3, 2009

127

United States District Court
Middle District of Florida
Ocala Division

Lamar Bernard Burno,
Plaintiff

v.

Secretary, Department of Corrections,
Defendant(s)

Case# 5:24-cv-559-TPB-PRL

## PETITION FOR WRIT OF HABEAS CORPUS

This Petition for Writ of Habeas Corpus is submitted by Lamar Bernard Burno, respectfully challenging his arrest and conviction due to prosecutorial misconduct, ineffective assistance of counsel, racial discrimination, and reliance on unverified accusations. Mr. Burno asserts that his conviction is a result of violations of his Constitutional rights, including due process and equal protection. He seeks relief from this Court, citing key federal cases supporting his claims.

### Grounds for Relief

1. **Fabricated Affidavit of Probable Cause**

The Florida Department of Law Enforcement (FDLE) initiated Mr. Burno's arrest based solely on an anonymous and unverified letter, violating due process. This letter, neither substantiated nor corroborated, served as the sole basis for probable cause:

- Mapp v. Ohio, 367 U.S. 643 (1961): Establishes the exclusionary rule, barring illegally obtained evidence in court. The FDLE's actions lack legitimate probable cause, rendering evidence inadmissible.
- Illinois v. Gates, 462 U.S. 213 (1983): Sets the standard for probable cause based on anonymous tips, requiring reliability and independent corroboration—criteria unmet in Mr. Burno's case.

2. **Improper Involvement of Pennsylvania Attorney General**

Unsubstantiated allegations were forwarded from the Florida Attorney General's Office to Pennsylvania, leading to action without sufficient investigation. This lack of due diligence contributed to Mr. Burno's wrongful prosecution:

- Rochin v. California, 342 U.S. 165 (1952): Holds that actions "shocking to the conscience" violate due process. The prosecution's lack of independent investigation constitutes a due process violation under this standard.

3. **Frivolous and Malicious Allegations by Lamont Bershawn**

Driven by jealousy, Lamont Bershawn filed false claims that lacked merit, leading Mr. Burno to surrender voluntarily. The lack of evidence underscores a failure in due process protections:

128

- Brady v. Maryland, 373 U.S. 83 (1963): The prosecution must disclose exculpatory evidence, but their acceptance of unverified claims and failure to investigate breaches Brady's mandate.

### 4. Ineffective Assistance of Counsel

Mr. Burno's counsel, Jaimie Washo, did not call essential witnesses, withheld military records, and offered no opening statement, failing Mr. Burno's right to effective counsel:

- Strickland v. Washington, 466 U.S. 668 (1984): Sets a two-part test for ineffective assistance of counsel: (1) deficient performance and (2) prejudice to the defense. Washo's deficiencies meet both criteria, undermining Mr. Burno's defense.
- Gideon v. Wainwright, 372 U.S. 335 (1963): Affirms the right to competent legal representation, which Mr. Burno was denied due to Washo's performance.

### 5. Prosecutorial Misconduct

After the original prosecutor recognized that no crime had been committed, subsequent prosecutor Ms. Popolo withheld exculpatory evidence and allowed false testimony:

- Kyles v. Whitley, 514 U.S. 419 (1995): States that suppressing material evidence affects trial outcomes, reinforcing the Brady doctrine. The prosecution's actions fit this description, violating Mr. Burno's due process rights.

### 6. Racial Discrimination and Threats by Law Enforcement

Mr. Burno faced threats and intimidation from law enforcement, including Chris DeLibro and Rus Edwards, who undermined his career and personal safety:

- Batson v. Kentucky, 476 U.S. 79 (1986): Prohibits racial discrimination in legal proceedings, supporting Mr. Burno's equal protection claim.
- Powell v. Alabama, 287 U.S. 45 (1932): Affirms that discriminatory practices during a trial process violate due process and equal protection under the Fourteenth Amendment.

### 7. Defamatory Testimony by Detective Broomes

Detective Broomes falsely testified that Mr. Burno was discharged from the military for pregnancy, defaming his character and violating his right to a fair trial:

- Napue v. Illinois, 360 U.S. 264 (1959): Holds that a conviction obtained through known false testimony by the prosecutor violates due process, fitting Mr. Burno's situation.

## Post-Trial Obstruction and Evidentiary Hearing

Following his conviction, Mr. Burno retained attorney Rajan Joshi and requested an evidentiary hearing before Judge Mark Nacke. During this hearing, Ms. Washo admitted to neglecting Mr. Burno's case, yet Judge Nacke obstructed justice by denying access to trial transcripts under the false claim that none existed.

- United States v. Agurs, 427 U.S. 97 (1976): Emphasizes the prosecution's duty to disclose material evidence, applicable here where access to trial records was wrongly denied.

## Fraudulent Use of Military Records by Prosecution

# WACKENHUT
# TRAINING INSTITUTE

PRESENTS THIS

## Certificate of Training Achievement

TO

**LAMAR B. BURNO**

FOR SUCCESSFUL COMPLETION OF THE

## Custom Protection Officer Training Program

AWARDED ON

INSTRUCTOR

AREA MANAGER

PRESIDENT AND
CHIEF OPERATING OFFICER

CUSTOM
WACKENHUT
PROTECTION
DIVISION

VICE PRESIDENT, TRAINING
WACKENHUT TRAINING INSTITUTE

Thank u kindly 4being who u r. Im the same way &
in my youth wouldve gladly accepted ur
"challenge"(have yet 2have anyone since losing
my innocence @17 "rock my world"-Lol!) but Im
2"seasoned" 2play those games anymore nor do I
desire 2. I think he was "fishing" 4info but was
unsuccessful. I sent an MMS pic msg (sexually
humorous) as I often do w/my friends that are
mature enuf 2handle that side of me 2show that Im
NOT always "SUPER SERIOUS &
SPIRITUAL"(I call it my "character balance").
After realizing what he was attempting 2do & that
his insistant proclaim 2 being single & wantin 2c
what I was made of wasnt workin; I calld him on it
by reminding him that his display of affection w/his
lady-friend said otherwise. He saw that he wasnt
gonna "charm" me into givin him my "cookies"
he began 2push u as a gr8 choice by sayin- ok, I
can see tht my brotha has won,again but Im cool
w/it besides he really likes u more anyway. Im
praying 4the best btwn u2 "Ms Heartbreaker"!
 Huh? Lol! My reply was we're cool & Id like it
2stay that way if/unless things change. I dont
create drama (esp btwn families) I watch it as
entertainment. Whateva (if anything beyond what
we're creating) happens Id prefer it stay w/us.
Hope this doesnt damage our "friendship"or cause
descension btwn u & him. Id like us 2grow but as
the woman I know my place & will follow ur lead
unless instructed otherwise. Be safe/Be blessed/
Stay sexy!

**THE WHITE HOUSE**
WASHINGTON

Congratulations on your achievement. Setting our sights high, we can meet our greatest aspirations and inspire those around us. You should take pride in your commitment, hard work, and accomplishments. I wish you all the best.

Sincerely,

## United States Senate
WASHINGTON, D. C.

ROBERT P. CASEY, JR.
PENNSYLVANIA

September 22, 2009

Dear Mr. Burno,

I want to offer my warmest congratulations upon your being recognized for your humanitarian service by The Preservation for Human Rights and Equality.

This recognition speaks to the high regard in which you are held by your colleagues and is a wonderful acknowledgment of the hard work, commitment and leadership you have shown throughout your life. Your lifetime of work helping others is truly exemplary.

Please accept my congratulations and best wishes on this well-deserved honor.

Sincerely,

Robert P. Casey, Jr.
United States Senator

Lamar Burno
1512 W. Church Rd
Wyncote, PA 19095

# THE SHAOLIN EXPERIENCE
# CREDD & STUDENT OATH

## THE SHAOLIN EXPERIENCE CREED

I am a student of The Shaolin Experience.
I walk the path of wisdom, discipline, and strength.

I train my body to endure,
My mind to focus,
And my spirit to rise,

I seek not to dominate,
But to defend,
Not to destrove.
But to preserve.

I will avoid conflict when I can.
But stand with courage when I must.

I will honor my teachers,
profect the innocent,
And lead with integrity.

In all things. I strive for balance—
Between power and peace.
Between motion and siillness,
Between force
and forgiveness.

This is my creed.
This is my calling.

## As a student of The Shaolin Experience, I solemnly swear.

— To respect my instructors, fellow students, and myself at all times.
— To use my skills only in the defense of truth, life, and justice.
— To train with honor, pattence and discipline—never arrogan-ee or pride.
— To uphold the principles of peace, humility, an self-con-trol.
— To grow in strength, but even more in wisdom.
— To be a living example of the art I study, both inside and outside the academy.

I am not trained to harm—I am trained to heal.

I am not taught to hate—I am guided by purpose.

This is my path.
I will live it with every

October 3, 2009

Dear Mr. Lamar Burno,

Please accept my warmest congratulations as you are honored by the Preservation for Human Rights and Equality and Faith United Church of the Living God for your selfless work on behalf of the residents in New Jersey and Pennsylvania.

Since 2006, you have dedicated your time and efforts as Commander of the Pennsylvania Chapter of the Guardian Angels. You worked tirelessly to train all members of Pennsylvania and New Jersey on numerous self-defense tactics, cooperated with law enforcement officials to solve crimes, campaigned against crime and gang violence, and assisted the elderly community.

You have truly displayed the combination of selflessness and compassion that is vital for community leaders through your numerous activities. I commend you for your honorable service to our country as a military police officer for seven years and to the community as an ordained Reverend since 1997.

As a United States Senator, I am committed to improving lives for those in my home state and across the nation. Once again, congratulations on tonight's recognition and best wishes in all your future endeavors.

Sincerely,

ROBERT MENENDEZ
United States Senator

136

Commonwealth of Pennsylvania

# Congratulatory Citation

**Whereas,** Lamar Bernard Burno is a native of the West Oak Lane section of Philadelphia, currently residing in Wyncote, PA, and;

**Whereas,** Lamar Bernard Burno excelled in his studies of criminal justice and law enforcement education at North Carolina Central University, and;

**Whereas,** Lamar Bernard Burno has served his country in the United States Army as an Infantryman and in Military Intelligence, and with the United States Army Reserves, Willow Grove, Montgomery County, Pennsylvania as a Military Police Officer, and;

**Whereas,** Lamar Bernard Burno protected the teachers, students, and facilities of the School District of Philadelphia by working as a Philadelphia School Police Officer, and;

**Whereas,** Lamar Bernard Burno has used his education and skills to provide security services to East Coast Investigations in Durham, North Carolina and The Wackenhut Corporation in Wyncote, Pennsylvania, and;

**Whereas,** Lamar Bernard Burno provides protective and security services to Romeo Entertainment in Wet Creek New Jersey, and On-Point Executive Protection in Wyncote, Pennsylvania, and;

**Whereas,** Lamar Bernard Burno has taught at Rome's Hung-Gar Kung Fu Academy 2 in Philadelphia, Pennsylvania, and is a Black Belt Instructor, and;

**Whereas,** Lamar Bernard Burno proudly and honorably serves his community as a member of The Guardian Angels, deterring crime in every capacity, and;

**Whereas,** Lamar Bernard Burno is an ordained Reverend in World Christianship Ministries, and a member of the Prudence Lodge 011 of Free and Accepted Masons Constituted under Warrant from the M.W. Prince Hall Grand of Pennsylvania, and;

**Now therefore be it resolved,** that The Honorable LeAnna M. Washington, serving the 4th Senatorial District in Northwest Philadelphia and Montgomery Counties, does hereby salute Lamar Bernard Burno on his accomplishments to date, with best wishes for continued success in future endeavors, and;

**Now directs,** that a copy of this citation be delivered to Lamar Bernard Burno on Sunday, October 8, 2006, at an event sponsored by Preservation for Human Rights and Equality.

*LeAnna M. Washington*

LeAnna M. Washington
State Senator, 4th District
Commonwealth of Pennsylvania

THE VICE PRESIDENT
WASHINGTON

March 9, 1993

Lamar Burno
1512 W. Church Road
Wyncote, PA 19095

Dear Mr. Burno:

Thank you for your interest in working for Vice-President Al
Gore. We appreciate your support of the Clinton-Gore
administration.

I have reviewed your resume and outstanding credentials. I will
keep you in mind in the event any suitable position becomes
available.

Thank you, once again, for your interest and support.

Sincerely,

Todd Campbell
Deputy Counsel and Director of Administration

138

Treasures of the Heart International Ministries
dba Crystal Rain Institute
115 Folly Ct., Fayetteville, NC 28356-1006
(910) 286-9436

December 22, 2020

Dear Honorable Judge,

Please accept this letter as a testament to the character of one Mr. Lamont Bershawn Burno. Your honor I received an inbox from Lamont in June of 2010 on a social Media platform named "TAGGED." He began talking about a ministry he wanted to get off the ground. He also said he was looking for a wife, and spoke of a reality show entitled "The Bishop's Wife." The ministry was named "I Found My Rib."

Your Honor, I helped as much as could from California. When I needed more information about the ministry he would become angry. I cautioned him to control his anger and vulgar language. I began to look into his "Bishopric." Well to my surprise, he was not a real Bishop in the Lord's Church, and the ministry "I Found My Rib" wasn't a real ministry in Wyncote, PA. When I confronted him about his flagrant lies, he slandered me, threatened me, and vowed to always make my life a living hell.

After being abused by him, and his girlfriend, I contacted the authorities. The Stanislaus County Sheriff's Department spoke with Lamont Burno, and determined from that conversation that he had in fact harassed me. I was given a report number; they also made contact with a Detective Mata from the Cheltenham PD.

In February of 2011, Lamont began to act very strange. He had started talking about his brother. I knew about his oldest brother, but he said he had a twin. This was out of the blue. He was angry, threatening and accusatory. Lamont said he wished his brother was dead and felt as if Lamar wanted his life. I hadn't met Lamar or Lamont in person at this point, as of today I've never met Lamont. I believe I had a conversation with Lamont on or about February 21, 2011 in which I received disrespect, names calling, threats and more.

I eventually received a call from Mr. Lamar Bernard Burno in May of 2012. We had a conversation, and he assured me that they had Lamont under some control at that time. Well, Lamont broke away from that control and began to destroy every life around him, especially Lamar. He has drug his brother through the ringer for no reason at all. Lamar has become his

140

November 10, 2009

Dear Mr. Burno:

I was recently informed that you were honored by the Preservation for Human Rights and Equality as well as Faith United Church of the Living God for all the good work you do for your community. Allow me the honor and privilege of congratulating you and thanking you for all your hard work.

Being a leader in the community often means espousing the ideals of servitude and self sacrifice. These are two ideals that are reflected in your years of service. It is fitting that you should be recognized for all you have done and continue to do.

On behalf of the United States Senate and the great Commonwealth of Pennsylvania I extend my thanks for a job well done.

My best.

Sincerely,

Arlen Specter

AS:kl

Mr. Lamar Burno
1827 Delhi Street
Philadelphia, PA 19136

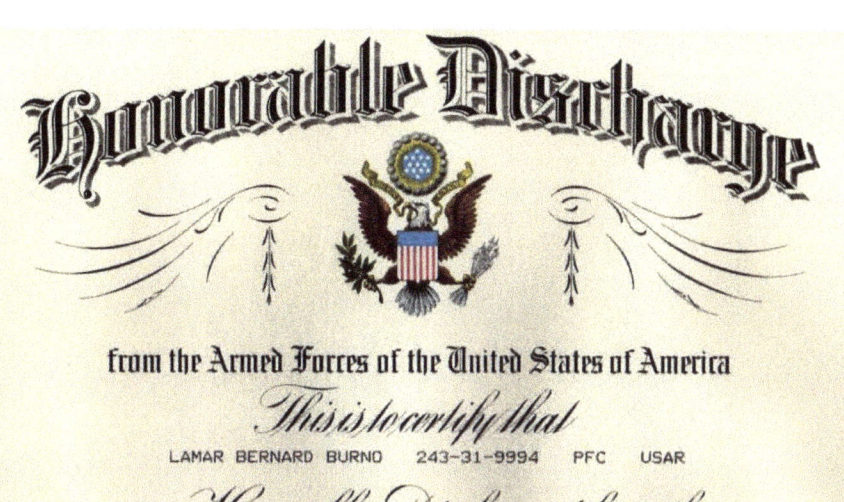

# Honorable Discharge

from the Armed Forces of the United States of America

This is to certify that

LAMAR BERNARD BURNO    243-31-9994    PFC    USAR

was Honorably Discharged from the

# United States Army

on the ___4TH___ day of ___FEBRUARY 2004___ This certificate is awarded as a testimonial of Honest and Faithful Service

Debra A. Cook

DEBRA A. COOK
COL, MS
COMMANDING

FORM NO. 256A 1 MAY 50

STATE OF NEW JERSEY
OFFICE OF THE GOVERNOR
P.O. BOX 001
TRENTON
08625
(609) 292-6000

JON S. CORZINE
GOVERNOR

August 15, 2009

**LAMAR BURNO**

Dear Mr. Burno:

I would like to extend congratulations as you are honored today.

Today's event honors your commitment to volunteering your time, talents and energy to those that need it most. Thank you for your outstanding service to the people of your community. Your willingness to go beyond what is required is truly appreciated. It is through the dedication of individuals like you that we may hope to build a better future for our citizens.

Again, congratulations on receiving this award, and best wishes for much success in your future endeavors.

Best wishes,

JON S. CORZINE

146

PRESENTED TO
LAMAR BURNO
FOR HIS BODYGUARD WORK
TO COMMEMORATE RIAA CERTIFIED
GOLD® SALES OF MORE THAN
500,000 COPIES OF THE
DREAMWORKS RECORDS
ALBUM, CASSETTE & CD
'GHETTO HYMNS'

147

# ELIZABETHTOWN POLICE DEPARTMENT
## UNIFORM PATROL DIVISION

**805 WEST BROAD STREET**
**P.O. BOX 1278**
**ELIZABETHTOWN, NORTH CAROLINA 28337**
**Chief of Police**
**Anthony T. Parrish**

TELEPHONE: 910-862-3125
FAX: 910-862-2743
E-MAIL:
police@elizabethtownnc.org
4/25/2024

On, 04/092024 Lamont Bershawn called the Elizabethtown Police Department to have a welfare check done on his brother Lamar Burno at 800 James St. When I arrived, Lamar was not home. A short while later I received a call from Burno stating his brother was making a big deal of a personal disagreement that they had. Burno stated that Lamont and himself agreed to break ties and never to speak again. Burno stated he was fine, and he was just moving on with his life and did not want any further contact with his brother Lamont. Burno stated that Lamont was doing this to be spiteful.

This letter was prepared for Mr Burno to document the incident on 04/09/2024.

Lt. McMichael
Elizabethtown Police Department

FILED
2024 APR 26 A 9 36
BLADEN CO. C.S.C.
BY

2/21/2020

148

# Commonwealth of Pennsylvania

# Congratulatory Citation

**Whereas,** Lamar Bernard Burno is a native of the West Oak Lane section of Philadelphia, currently residing in Wyncote, PA, and;

**Whereas,** Lamar Bernard Burno excelled in his studies of criminal justice and law enforcement education at North Carolina Central University, and;

**Whereas,** Lamar Bernard Burno has served his country in the United States Army as an Infantryman and in Military Intelligence, and with the United States Army Reserves, Willow Grove, Montgomery County, Pennsylvania as a Military Police Officer, and;

**Whereas,** Lamar Bernard Burno protected the teachers, students, and facilities of the School District of Philadelphia by working as a Philadelphia School Police Officer, and;

**Whereas,** Lamar Bernard Burno has used his education and skills to provide security services to East Coast Investigations in Durham, North Carolina and The Wackenhut Corporation in Wyncote, Pennsylvania, and;

**Whereas,** Lamar Bernard Burno provides protective and security services to Romeo Entertainment in Wet Creek New Jersey, and On-Point Executive Protection in Wyncote, Pennsylvania, and;

**Whereas,** Lamar Bernard Burno has taught at Rome's Hung-Gar Kung Fu Academy 2 in Philadelphia, Pennsylvania, and is a Black Belt Instructor, and;

**Whereas,** Lamar Bernard Burno proudly and honorably serves his community as a member of The Guardian Angels, deterring crime in every capacity, and;

**Whereas,** Lamar Bernard Burno is an ordained Reverend in World Christianship Ministries, and a member of the Prudence Lodge 011 of Free and Accepted Masons Constituted under Warrant from the M.W. Prince Hall Grand of Pennsylvania, and;

**Now therefore be it resolved,** that The Honorable LeAnna M. Washington, serving the 4th Senatorial District in Northwest Philadelphia and Montgomery Counties, does hereby salute Lamar Bernard Burno on his accomplishments to date, with best wishes for continued success in future endeavors, and;

**Now directs,** that a copy of this citation be delivered to Lamar Bernard Burno on Sunday, October 8, 2006, at an event sponsored by Preservation for Human Rights and Equality.

*LeAnna M. Washington*

LeAnna M. Washington
State Senator, 4th District
Commonwealth of Pennsylvania

149

ARLEN SPECTER
UNITED STATES SENATOR
WASHINGTON, D.C. 20510

November 10, 2009

Dear Mr. Burno:

I was recently informed that you were honored by the Preservation for Human Rights and Equality as well as Faith United Church of the Living God for all the good work you do for your community. Allow me the honor and privilege of congratulating you and thanking you for all your hard work.

Being a leader in the community often means espousing the ideals of servitude and self sacrifice. These are two ideals that are reflected in your years of service. It is fitting that you should be recognized for all you have done and continue to do.

On behalf of the United States Senate and the great Commonwealth of Pennsylvania I extend my thanks for a job well done.

My best.

Sincerely,

Arlen Specter

AS/dd

Mr. Lamar Burno
1827 Dallas Street
Philadelphia, PA 19126

BACCALAUREATE CATEGORY, 3 SEMESTER HOURS FOR FIELD EXPERIENCE IN MANAGEMENT.

| Military Occupational Specialties Held: | 95B10 | Primary | From: 08/2001 | To: 01/2004 |
|---|---|---|---|---|
| | 95B10 | Duty | | |

Military Occupational Specialty Group 95B

ACE Guide Number

Title: Military Police

MOS 95B-004

SQT (Thru Oct 1991)/SDT (Nov 1991 thru Feb 1995) Taken: None

Description of 95B10: ENFORCES TRAFFIC REGULATIONS AND LAW AND ORDER; EXERCISES MILITARY CONTROL AND DISCIPLINE AND GUARDS PRISONERS OF WAR; RESPONSIBLE FOR TRAFFIC ACCIDENT INVESTIGATION; PROVIDES PHYSICAL SECURITY FOR DESIGNATED INDIVIDUALS, INSTALLATIONS, FACILITIES, AND EQUIPMENT; MAINTAINS TRAFFIC CONTROL AND ENFORCES TRAFFIC REGULATIONS AND SAFETY; PARTICIPATES IN CIVIL DISTURBANCES AND RIOT CONTROL OPERATIONS; RESPONSIBLE FOR LAW ENFORCEMENT INVESTIGATIONS; PERFORMS FOOT AND MOTORIZED PATROL AND APPLIES CRIME PREVENTION MEASURES; PREPARES MILITARY POLICE REPORTS INCLUDING SWORN STATEMENTS AND PROCESSES EVIDENCE.

ACE Credit Recommendation for 95B10: IN THE LOWER-DIVISION BACCALAUREATE/ASSOCIATE DEGREE CATEGORY, 3 SEMESTER HOURS IN PATROL OPERATIONS. (NOTE: THIS RECOMMENDATION FOR SKILL LEVEL 10 IS VALID FOR THE DATES 3/86-9/91 ONLY). (NOTE: THIS RECOMMENDATION FOR SKILL LEVEL 10 IS VALID FOR THE DATES 3/86-9/91 ONLY).

Special Qualification Identifiers: None

Additional Skill Identifiers: None

| Other Learning Experience |
|---|
| THIS SECTION PROVIDES THE ACADEMIC AND BUSINESS COMMUNITIES WITH A RECORD OF THE SOLDIER'S LEARNING EXPERIENCES. COURSES LISTED MAY FALL INTO ONE OF THE FOLLOWING CATEGORIES: THOSE THAT ACE WILL NEVER EVALUATE FOR COLLEGE CREDIT, THOSE THAT ARE PENDING EVALUATION, AND THOSE THAT ARE EVALUATED BUT ARE NOT CURRENTLY COMPUTER COMPATIBLE. EVENTUALLY MOST OF THE LEARNING EXPERIENCES IN THE SECOND AND THIRD CATEGORIES WILL BE INCLUDED IN THE MAIN BODY OF THE TRANSCRIPT. WE RECOMMEND REVIEW OF THE LISTINGS WITH THE SOLDIER TO DETERMINE THE APPROPRIATENESS OF THE EXPERIENCES TO THE SOLDIER'S PROGRAM OF STUDY OR EMPLOYMENT. |

None

151

OFFICE OF THE MAYOR

CITY OF TRENTON, NEW JERSEY 08608

DOUGLAS H. PALMER
MAYOR

609-989-3030

September 9, 2009

Dear Mr. Lamar Burno,

On behalf of the city of Trenton, I take this opportunity to congratulate you for your outstanding service and dedication to the citizens of New Jersey.

I join the community at large in recognizing your humanitarian, educational and diverse strengths. Individuals of all ages have been encouraged and inspired by the continuous personal services you have provided. On behalf of the people of Trenton, I thank you for your love and dedication to enhance and improve the lives of the citizens of New Jersey. May God continue to bless you most abundantly as you continue to serve the community with love and dedication.

Again, congratulations, God bless and keep up the good work!

Sincerely,

Douglas H. Palmer
Mayor

152

The prosecution unlawfully retained and misrepresented Mr. Burno's military records, withholding exculpatory information crucial to his defense. This action constitutes prosecutorial misconduct:

- Brady v. Maryland, 373 U.S. 83 (1963): Requires full disclosure of exculpatory evidence, which was breached through false representations and withholding of military records.

## Relief Sought

1. Immediate dismissal of the charge of uttering a forged document.
2. Compensation for damages, including lost career opportunities and earnings following his successful completion of the Florida SOCE Exam.
3. Formal apologies from the states of Florida and Pennsylvania for proceeding with charges without thorough investigation.
4. Issuance of a certified Florida law enforcement status from the FDLE and a certified copy of Mr. Burno's SOCE Exam passing score.

**Respectfully submitted,**

Lamar Bernard Burno
800 James St
Elizabethtown, NC 28337
910-709-3749

## Certificate of Service

I, Lamar Burno, hereby certify that a true and correct copy of the foregoing has been furnished by U.S. Mail to the Florida Department of Corrections, 501 S Calhoun St, Tallahassee, FL 32399, and to the U.S. Attorney's Office, 400 North Tampa St., Suite 3200, Tampa, FL 33602, on this 31st day of October, 2024.

# On Point Executive Protection

The elite in executive protection

DEPARTMENT OF THE ARMY

CERTIFICATE OF ACHIEVEMENT

AWARDED TO

PVT LAMAR B. BURNO

COMPANY B, 4TH BATTALION, 30TH INFANTRY
UNITED STATES ARMY INFANTRY TRAINING CENTER
FORT BENNING, GEORGIA

FOR ACHIEVING A SCORE OF 40 OUT OF 40 IN BASIC
RIFLE MARKSMANSHIP FOR THE CYCLE 3-92

31 January 1992

M. C. REED
LTC, IN
Commanding

DA FORM 2442, 1 JUN 81

| File No. | | |
|---|---|---|
| 24CR290751-080 | Law Enforcement Case No. | LID No. |

## CRIMINAL SUMMONS

### THE STATE OF NORTH CAROLINA VS.

Name And Address Of Defendant
LAMAR BERNARD BURNO
800 JAMES ST.

ELIZABETHTOWN    NC    28337
Bladen COUNTY        910-709-3749

**STATE OF NORTH CAROLINA**

BLADEN _____ County

In The General Court Of Justice
District Court Division

| Race | Sex | Date Of Birth | Age | OFFENSE(S) (see AOC-CR-113 Continuation(s) for charging text) | | |
|---|---|---|---|---|---|---|
| B | M | 2/11/1973 | 51 | | | |

| Count No. | Offense | Offense In Violation Of G.S. | Offense Code |
|---|---|---|---|
| 1 | M - COMMUNICATING THREATS | 14-277.1 | 5328 |

Name Of Defendant's Employer

Date Of Offense
04/21/2024

☐ Misdemeanor Offense Which Requires Fingerprinting Per Fingerprint Plan

Complainant Name (and address, if Complainant is an officer)
LAMONT BURNO

Witness Information

**TO THE DEFENDANT:**
I, the undersigned, find that there is probable cause to believe that on or about the date of offense shown and in the county named above you unlawfully, willfully, and feloniously did commit the offense(s) set forth above and on the attached AOC-CR-113 Continuation(s), which is (are) incorporated by reference. This act(s) was in violation of the law referred to in this Criminal Summons. This Criminal Summons is issued upon information furnished under oath by the complainant listed. You are ORDERED to appear before the Court at the location, date and time indicated below to answer to the charge(s). If you fail to appear, an order for your arrest may be issued and/or you may be held in CONTEMPT OF COURT. Arrest and/or contempt for failure to appear is in addition to any sentence or penalty which may be imposed for the offense(s) charged.

☒ The undersigned finds the following cause to set a court date more than one month from the issue of this summons:
NEXT NON OFFICER COURT DATE

| Date Issued | Name Of Issuing Official | Signature | | |
|---|---|---|---|---|
| 04/24/2024 | R. KINLAW | Robert Kinlaw | ☒ Magistrate ☐ Deputy CSC ☐ Assistant CSC ☐ Clerk Of Superior Court | ☐ District Court Judge ☐ Superior Court Judge |

| Location Of Court | Court Date | Court Time |
|---|---|---|
| Bladen Co. Courthouse, Courtroom 1 | 05/30/2024 | 9:30 AM |

### WAIVER OF PROBABLE CAUSE HEARING

The undersigned defendant, with the consent of his/her attorney, waives the right to a probable cause hearing.

| Date Waived | Signature Of Defendant | Name Of Attorney | Signature Of Attorney |
|---|---|---|---|
| | | | |

(Over)
Defendant

AOC-CR-113, Rev. 3/23, © 2023 Administrative Office of the Courts

VRA Case

IN THE CIRCUIT COURT OF THE FIFTH JUDICIAL CIRCUIT,
IN AND FOR LAKE COUNTY, FLORIDA

CASE NO. 2013-CF-1432

STATE OF FLORIDA

v.

LAMAR B. BURNO,

        Defendant

_____/

## ORDER DENYING DEFENDANT'S REQUEST

THIS CAUSE having come before this Court on the Defendant's request to receive an official copy of the "Notes of Testimony" for this case, and the Court, having considered the request and the Court file, is not aware of the existence of "Notes of Testimony" in this case.

It is therefore, ORDERED AND ADJUDGED that the Defendant's request to receive an official copy of the "Notes of Testimony" is **DENIED.**

DONE AND ORDERED at the Lake County Judicial Center, Tavares, Lake County, Florida, this 29th day of June, 2016.

                                              _____

                                          MARK A. NACKE, CIRCUIT JUDGE

Copies to: AS  6/30

Office of the State Attorney
Tavares, Florida

Lamar Burno
800 James Street
Elizabethtown, North Carolina 28337

2016 JUN 29 A 10: 56
CLERK OF CIRCUIT
AND COUNTY COURTS
LAKE COUNTY
TAVARES, FL.

1

157

**LAMAR BURNO**

*Executive Producer*

www.ingramcontent.com/pod-product-compliance
Lightning Source LLC
Chambersburg PA
CBHW051624120626
46551CB00014B/1921

* 9 7 9 8 9 9 9 3 7 3 5 1 9 *